WRITE WITH CONFIDENCE

SHATTER SELF-LIMITING BELIEFS AND FINISH YOUR BOOK

LISA FELLINGER

Author Photo by Jessica Stewart Photography

Print edition ISBN 979-8-9898829-2-2

Digital edition ISBN 979-8-9898829-3-9

First Edition: June 2025

Published by Bailey Marie Press

www.lisafellinger.com

"Our only limitations are the ones we set up in our own minds."
    -Napoleon Hill

CONTENTS

INTRODUCTION

If writing a book is on your bucket list, you're certainly not alone. According to one study, 80% of Americans want to write a book someday. And if you haven't started writing that book yet, you're not alone either. Of those 80% of people who want to write a book, only 15% have actually started—and just 8% have finished.[i]

These numbers aren't surprising to me because writing a book is hard work, and challenging tasks threaten our self-esteem. And when something threatens our self-esteem, we tend to avoid it. Our brains will do Olympic-level gymnastics to keep us from engaging in that task, including convincing us that things are true which simply aren't or telling us we have "writer's block" when we're really just afraid to put our words out into the world.

While these stats might sound discouraging, if you're reading this book, you've already taken a giant first step in overcoming the mental blocks that are holding you back from writing the book you've always dreamed of. You're one huge step closer to actually writing a book than many of those 80%

because you recognize that writing a book isn't as simple as waiting until you have more time and hoping inspiration magically shows up.

If you're here, you likely already have an inkling that something within *you* has been keeping you from writing that book.

I strongly believe that writing a book is much more about mastering your mindset than being a gifted writer. Writing is a learnable skill. While we're all born with a certain level of writing talent, I fully believe that if you're determined to become a better writer, it's absolutely possible. But even if you're the most talented writer in the world with an exceptionally compelling book idea, if you can't manage to sit down at your desk and write the words, you'll never finish your manuscript.

This book is for you if you've dreamed of writing a book your entire life, but something always seems to hold you back. Maybe you can never fully settle on a story idea. Maybe you never seem to find the time to commit to writing it. Maybe every time you sit down at your computer or with your notebook, you freeze up. You ask yourself, *"What am I doing? I can't write a book."*

After all, you're not a writer. Other people are. But you're not.

If those sound like the kind of thoughts that run through your mind when you think about writing, you're in the right place. I've got you.

I've been a writer my whole life. I remember being too young to fully read *Little House on the Prairie* but holding the book in my hands and telling myself that would be me one day—I'd write a book and hold it in my hands, just like Laura Ingalls Wilder. I've had other career ambitions over the years, but the one thing that remained constant was my dream to one day see my name on the cover of a book. And all these years later, I published my debut novel just after my 36th birthday.

I was lucky to have supportive people in my life throughout the years. I had elementary school teachers who praised and encouraged my love for writing. I had parents who never made me feel silly for dreaming of becoming a published author. I have friends and colleagues who support my writing, and I've intentionally sought out a community of writers that I involve myself with who understand the highs and lows of the writing life. Having people in my life who support and understand my writing has given me a huge advantage—one that, sadly, I know many writers don't have.

But even with the support of family and friends, it's often the writer themselves holding them back from pursuing this dream. All too often, it's the lies we've come to believe about who we are and what we're capable of that keep us from sitting down and writing a book. It's the excuses we've come to rely on as crutches that keep us from doing something we may have dreamed about since we first started reading stories. It's *us* standing in the way of our own success.

But here's the good news: if we're the ones holding ourselves back from writing, then that means we also have the power to overcome whatever mental blocks are standing in our way and finally write the damn book. It might take some hard work, it might require some brutal honesty, and it might involve a tissue box or two, but the power to let go of what's holding us back lies solidly within ourselves. And with this book, my goal is to shed some light on what those obstacles might be and give you tools to overcome them.

I never intended to write a book like this. I'm a fiction writer and never pictured myself writing nonfiction, let alone a book about writing, but my career took a winding turn, and now I feel this is a book I *need* to write. But if you want to talk about imposter syndrome (and we will), trust me: when the idea for this book first came to me, I had a full-blown case. After all, who was I to tell other people how to overcome their self-limiting beliefs and write a book?

And then I did exactly what I'll tell you to do later in this book. I sat down and wrote out my credentials. And by credentials, I don't mean pieces of paper that say I'm qualified. I mean real-life experiences that give me the perspective to speak on these topics.

So, what are those credentials, you might be wondering?

As I mentioned, I'm a fiction writer, and while I've been writing in some capacity my entire life, I've been writing seriously (e.g., studying craft books, joining writing communities, taking workshops, and finishing manuscripts) for over a decade. I'm a professionally trained developmental editor and book coach and work with writers in this capacity daily. And I have a background in both mental health counseling and life coaching, which gives me a solid foundation to draw from when addressing the complex emotional aspects that often arise when a person wants to write but can't seem to make it happen.

As a book coach and editor, my goal is to help writers feel more confident in their abilities and to own the title of "writer." I strive to help my coaching clients overcome the limiting beliefs that interfere with their ability to write their book. And my hope for this book is to encourage even more writers—to give them the confidence to finally get out of their own way, believe in their writing abilities, and get their book written.

So, if you're ready to take an honest, hard look at what's stopping you from pursuing this dream you've been setting aside for months, years, or even decades, then you're in the right place. While it may not be fun to recognize that your own self-limiting beliefs have been holding you back, doing the work to identify and overcome them can open up the space for you to finally sit down and write.

No more saying *"one day"* you'll write a book. Today is the day.

Let's dig in.

WHAT'S REALLY STOPPING YOU FROM WRITING A BOOK?

WRITING A NOVEL IS UNDENIABLY HARD WORK. CRAFTING a story that's an average of 80,000 to 100,000 words with a complex and complete character arc, a plot that flows logically, and that allows readers to connect emotionally to our characters is no small feat. It requires significant time and energy to not only get words down but also to learn about writing craft, explore publication options, and connect with other writers.

If you've picked up this book, it's likely that you've either attempted to write a novel before and given up or you've been dreaming of writing one for a while but haven't managed to start. Perhaps you've told yourself that "one day" you'll write a book, but today isn't the day because...insert reason here.

There are countless reasons we give for not beginning our writing journey: work is busy, we're pursuing a degree, we have young kids, we have older kids, retirement is around the corner, so I'll wait until then...the list can go on and on. And on. These reasons sound perfectly logical on the surface. After all, writing a book is a huge undertaking, so it makes sense to hold off until things are a little less chaotic, until it's the "right moment."

But here's the thing: it's unlikely it will ever feel like the perfect moment to start writing. Life rarely becomes less chaotic. Just as we finish our degree, we embark on a new career. Then we have children, and it's hard to write with young kids around, but then as they get older, they have other needs that keep us up at all hours. Then the kids leave for college, and we retire, but now our aging parents need assistance throughout the day.

See what I mean?

There's no perfect time to start writing a book. It's going to be a difficult task no matter when we begin. But the first step towards overcoming the mental obstacles standing between us and writing the book of our dreams is recognizing that most (if not all) of the reasons we've told ourselves—and perhaps others—about why we can't start writing now are nothing more than excuses.

So, what's really stopping you from writing a book? Let's explore.

Writing is Hard

If you're anything like me, you had visions as a kid of grown-up you happily sitting at a computer as words effortlessly appeared on the screen. You dreamed of publishers knocking at your door to publish your book and negotiating movie rights. You imagined book readings and signings filled with readers eager to hear your thoughts and purchase your book.

And if you've been around any writers at all, you know that being a writer rarely looks like this. Sure, there are days when the writing flows easily, but more often are the days when you have to force yourself to sit at the desk and stay there until you make some progress. There are days when you write 1,000 words only to delete them all the next day. And there are days when you wonder why you even started this process and if your story idea even works. Those are the days when writing feels like anything but a dream.

Writing is undoubtedly hard, but using this as an excuse not to start is like saying you won't go to college because it will be challenging, or you won't play a sport because it will be physically demanding. It's hard, but it's always going to be hard. Whether you start writing today or three years from now, it will still be hard. But if you start today, in three years, you'll have made progress toward becoming a stronger writer.

The problem is that anything that feels hard automatically triggers our brains to become defensive. Our brains will do anything to keep us from confronting things that feel challenging and scary. Unfortunately for us, our brains don't know the difference between something dangerous and something that may be hard but rewarding.

This is where self-limiting beliefs come into play. The moment our brain senses that what we're about to attempt is difficult, it tries everything it can to dissuade us, including telling us that we simply can't for various reasons that seem logical. But in reality, we need to fight back against our brain's instincts. Just because writing is hard doesn't mean it's not worthwhile. Just because it's hard doesn't mean it's not a life dream we hope to accomplish.

Self-Limiting Beliefs

Self-limiting beliefs are convictions we hold about ourselves or the world that limit our ability to succeed. They can be hard to catch because they're often so ingrained in our minds that we accept them as facts rather than opinions.

Self-limiting beliefs are anything you tell yourself about your abilities or worth that prevent you from pursuing a goal. Examples include telling yourself you're not smart enough, you're not good enough, you don't deserve to do this, or you don't have enough time.

These beliefs stem from various sources, but they're often rooted in our early childhood. Because we're so vulnerable in our formative years, the experiences we have and the things we're told about ourselves tend to be accepted as fact without much questioning, and those beliefs take root deeply and tend to stick around. As the years go by, these beliefs then manifest in different ways.

Self-limiting beliefs are often so ingrained in our thinking that we don't even notice them sabotaging us. Since we tend to accept them as fact without question, they crop up and we just roll with them because we don't realize we can and *should* be questioning these thoughts. Because they're often automatic, identifying them takes a concerted effort.

However, the positive side is that since these thoughts reside solely within our minds, we have the power to change them. While some factors affecting our writing may feel out of our control—such as working a day job to pay the bills or dealing with a newborn's sleep schedule—self-limiting beliefs are entirely within our control to change. That doesn't mean they're *easy* to change, but it does mean it's doable.

Self-limiting beliefs can manifest in our writing in various ways. Sometimes, these beliefs are explicitly tied to our writing. For example, we might think we're not good at writing, so why bother? Or we might fear failure and wonder what will happen if our book flops.

But sometimes these beliefs go deeper than just writing and connect to deeply held convictions about ourselves. An example of this is feeling like we're not worthy of the time and energy needed to pursue a new venture, such as writing. We might believe that taking time away from our children to write is selfish. While these beliefs do impact our writing, they're more pervasive and affect other areas of our lives beyond just writing. These kinds of beliefs tend to be more difficult to overcome since they've often become entrenched in our belief system. But once we know what to look for and can identify these self-limiting beliefs, we can then determine how to tackle them.

Why You Need to Address Your Self-Limiting Beliefs

While it's easy to think that to get more writing done, you should spend time learning about craft or forcing yourself to stay at your writing desk until the words finally come, the truth is that addressing your mental blocks is the best place to start. This is always where I begin with any new book coaching client.

Why is addressing these beliefs so important? Because no matter how talented a writer you are, if you're holding onto self-limiting beliefs that tell you that your writing is worthless, that you should be doing something more productive, or that you're not good enough to become a published author, then you'll keep hitting the same wall. No matter how many hours you sit in front of your computer, you won't finish your manuscript if, deep down, you don't believe you can.

While some writers may be born with more natural talent, writing is also a highly learnable skill. There are countless books, courses, workshops, and conferences to learn how to craft better scenes, how to create a compelling character arc, and how to create plots readers will resonate with. But focusing on craft before you've addressed the thoughts telling you that you *can't* do this, before you believe that your story matters and that you're worthy of committing time to your writing, is putting the cart before the horse.

Ultimately, you are your biggest opposition to completing your book.

Our mindset and beliefs about ourselves are the foundation we build upon when working toward any goal, but especially a goal as big and personal as writing a book. Addressing your mental blocks might not feel as exciting as crafting characters or building story worlds, but doing this internal work first clears the path and allows for your writing sessions to be smoother and more productive. Instead of sitting down to write and wasting time and energy wrestling with your own negative thoughts, you can focus on your story.

Performing a Self-Evaluation

One of the first things I suggest to writers struggling to get words on the page is to spend some time conducting a self-evaluation. This doesn't have to feel clinical or rigid, but it should be honest. The goal is to get clear on what's holding you back from writing and to take inventory of the challenges—both tangible and emotional—that are making it hard to create and stick to a writing routine.

The purpose of a self-evaluation is to identify the blocks that are standing between you and your writing goals.

Tangible blocks are usually the easier ones to spot. These might include other demands on your time, such as a job, child-care, or ongoing responsibilities that take up big chunks of your week. But tangible blocks can also be less obvious. For instance, your health might be an impediment to your ability to write, either in the current moment or chronically. When we're not physically healthy, it can be hard to focus on our writing.

Another tangible block might be your writing environment. While some writers can work just about anywhere, others need a specific setup to feel their best creatively. It can also be challenging to do creative work in the same space we do other work, so even if you have a desk setup at home but you spend most of your time there working from home for your day job, you might find this space isn't suitable for you to do creative work at.

Then there are the emotional blocks, which are often even more powerful but harder to identify. These are the blocks that don't necessarily steal your time, but also steal your energy, your focus, or your belief in yourself.

Emotional blocks are often self-limiting beliefs. But they can also take other forms: battling depression or anxiety, navigating uncertainty like a job change or a move, or picking up extra responsibilities around the house while your partner can't pitch in as much. These may not as obviously take away from our time to write as the tangible blocks, but they often leave you feeling mentally drained. So even if you *technically* have time to write, you don't have the mental capacity.

My favorite way to perform a self-evaluation is through journaling. Some people prefer making a list of their blocks. Others find it more helpful to simply write about their day and see what surfaces. Whatever approach works for you is fine. The point is to be honest and curious—not judgmental.

To help you with this, I've compiled some specific prompts to get you started.

Identifying Tangible Blocks:

- What does a typical day or week look like for you? Where are you currently fitting in writing time, or where could you potentially carve some out?
- When you do sit down to write, do you feel physically or mentally exhausted?
- Do you schedule time to write, or are you hoping inspiration and free time will magically appear?

- Is your writing space comfortable and inviting? Does it help you feel creative?
- Are your writing goals clear and manageable, or do they feel overwhelming and vague?
- Are there tools or routines missing that would make it easier to write?
- What other responsibilities or roles are competing with your time and energy to write?

Identifying Emotional Blocks:

- What thoughts come up right before a writing session? Do they ever convince you to skip writing?
- Do you expect your writing to be "good" right away?
- Are you comparing yourself to other writers (consciously or subconsciously)?
- Do you consider yourself a "real" writer? Why or why not?
- What stories are you telling yourself about your abilities, time, or worth?
- When in the past have you stopped writing altogether? What was happening in your life at that time?
- What are you afraid might happen if you *do* finish your book?
- What are you afraid might happen if you *don't*?
- Are you worried about being judged by readers, family, friends, or even yourself?

Taking the time to explore these questions honestly can reveal a great deal about how you're prioritizing your writing, how your daily routines support or sabotage your goals, and what fears or beliefs may be holding you back. It might feel uncomfortable to hold up that mirror, but it's essential.

Naming what stands between you and your ideal writing life is the first empowering step toward clearing the path and giving yourself the best chance to finally reach your writing goals.

2

YOU ARE A REAL WRITER

WHEN I STARTED MY BOOK COACHING BUSINESS, THE FIRST blog post I shared was about owning the title of "writer." I chose that topic intentionally because it's one of the biggest obstacles many of us—yes, even the published writers—struggle with.

Calling ourselves a writer, whether silently to ourselves or aloud to others, can feel incredibly vulnerable. It can bring up all sorts of doubts and insecurities, including the dreaded imposter syndrome. Declaring that we are, in fact, writers shines a spotlight on us. It's an act of bravery, one that exposes a life-long dream to the world and invites others to have opinions about it. And people always seem to have opinions about writers, don't they? It often feels easier to stay quiet, to keep our dream of becoming an author to ourselves.

But if we can't identify as a writer, if we can't boldly claim that title, we'll struggle to take our writing seriously. Mindset is essential when tackling a huge goal like writing a book, and if we don't believe we deserve to call ourselves writers, we'll struggle to show up at our desks and do the work. Self-fulfilling prophecies are real, and by avoiding the identity of "writer," we set ourselves up to continually fail at achieving that goal.

What Exactly is a Writer?

More often than not, our struggle with calling ourselves writers comes down to one simple thing: not realizing that what we're doing already qualifies us as one.

First, let's clarify the difference between being a writer and being a published author. The definitions are straightforward—a writer is someone who writes, and a published author is someone who has published their writing. Many writers hesitate to claim the title because they worry they're pretending to be something they're not. But calling yourself a writer has nothing to do with whether or not your words have made it into print.

Even once they understand that difference, though, many writers still hesitate to own the title. Why? Because they have a very specific, idealized image in their mind of what a writer looks like.

Often, when we think of a writer, we picture someone sitting at a desk from 9 to 5, weaving a beautiful story full of interesting characters and gorgeous language. This mythical writer receives an advance before they've even started their next manuscript. They have deadlines, lunch dates with their agent, book tours, and adoring fans lining up to hear them read from their brilliant books.

But here's the thing: most writers don't look like that. In fact, of the many writers I know, not one has a life like this.

The writers I know are writing alongside full-time jobs, raising kids, supporting aging parents, etc. They're sneaking their writing into the margins of an already full life. Even the ones writing full-time aren't living that "ideal" version of a writer's life.

Published authors certainly didn't start that way—they started with only a blank page and a hope that someone, some-day, would read their story.

And most writers, no matter how long they've been writing, have struggled with imposter syndrome at some point. That inner critic doesn't discriminate. It whispers that we're not real writers because we don't match the image we've constructed in our minds.

But a writer is simply someone who writes.

This feels like such a simple, obvious statement, and yet I can't tell you the number of times I've told this to someone and watched their face change as they let this sink in, as they realize that I'm not being ridiculous when I call them a writer, and they shouldn't feel that way either.

In all our dreaming about what it would be like to "be a writer," we often lose sight of what the title actually means. We get so caught up in imagining an ideal writing life that we fail to recognize we're already living a very real one.

If you write, you're a writer. It's as simple as that.

Right?

Owning the Title of Writer

We've all been there. You're at a party, an event, or even just standing in the school pick up line, and someone strikes up a casual conversation. Sooner or later, they ask: "What do you do?"

One of the most dreaded questions for a writer—second only, perhaps, to "What's your book about?"

I could go on about how a person isn't defined solely by their career, but like it or not, this question has become a socially accepted shortcut to getting to know someone. And while we can't control what others ask, we *can* control how we respond.

The dreaded "what do you do" question tends to bring up all kinds of feelings: imposter syndrome, self-consciousness, embarrassment—it brings it all to the surface. But those feelings aren't there because of the question itself. They're there because, deep down, whether we recognize it consciously or not, we're uncomfortable calling ourselves a writer. When someone asks what we do, and we haven't made peace with that title, it can feel threatening. If we haven't yet figured out what being a writer means for us, the question will trigger our insecurities and put us on the defensive. Sharing that we write also opens the door to more questions, ones we may not feel ready to answer.

Another reason this question can spark our defenses is that while we might have a straightforward answer to the question (i.e., "I'm an accountant!"), if we're *also* a writer, that simple answer doesn't feel like the whole truth. But adding in, "I also write," can feel awkward or vulnerable. It's a lose-lose: keep it simple but feel like you're hiding part of yourself or tell the truth and risk feeling like a fraud.

I'll never forget the first time I called myself a writer to someone who wasn't my family or a close friend. I was in a graduate school class, and we were discussing the demands of the program and what challenges we were facing. I don't know what was going through my mind that night, but the first thing that tumbled out of my mouth was, "I'm a writer, and I miss having time for my writing."

Now, at this time, I hadn't even completed a manuscript. I'd been writing stories my whole life, but I was on a path to become a counselor. My plan was to finish school, get a "real" job (whatever that meant), and then I'd have time to focus on my writing. I didn't consciously consider myself a writer in that moment. And I was mortified that I'd just declared myself one in this room full of serious, career-minded graduate students. *What was I thinking?*

Then my professor raised his eyebrows and said, "Wow! What do you write? I also write!"

I don't remember the rest of the conversation. I was too focused on the fact that I'd just pretended to be a real writer out loud, in public, in front of someone who I'd just learned had actually published books. I'm sure my cheeks were as red as an apple.

I don't know if any of my classmates remember that moment. But I sure do. Because that was the first time I truly claimed the title of writer. And it happened when I least expected it.

That moment didn't spark me to take immediate action, quit school, and decide to write full-time. But it stuck with me. In the back of my mind was the realization that even though I was in full pursuit of a different career, being a writer was still the thing that mattered most to me. And I think that moment was a quiet nudge from my subconscious that my real purpose might lie elsewhere.

It's gotten easier to tell people I'm a writer over the years. But even now, with a published book under my belt, it still feels a little vulnerable. I still have to remind myself that I am a writer, and I have no reason to feel ashamed sharing that.

Because here's the truth: we can't confidently tell others we're writers until we're comfortable telling *ourselves*. Until we can say "I write" without immediately qualifying it ("It's just a hobby," or "But I haven't published anything yet"), it will always feel intimidating to share.

So, how do we get comfortable with calling ourselves writers?

Practice.

I know it feels silly, but look yourself in the mirror and say, "I'm a writer." Say it again. And again. The more you do it, the less awkward it feels.

Sometimes, it's just about finding words that don't feel clunky. Coming up with a short script can be helpful. That way, when someone asks what you do, you're prepared—you've already decided what you feel comfortable sharing and how.

But if you keep practicing and it still feels hard, it might be more than just needing the right words. If this is the case, pay attention to what thoughts or feelings come up when you say, "I'm a writer." Do you feel the urge to qualify it? Do you worry it sounds pretentious? Are you biting your tongue, waiting to be called a fraud?

These thoughts are clues. They reveal the mental blocks standing between you and the writing life you want. And once you identify those blocks, you can begin to work through them to finally feel confident calling yourself a writer.

A Note About Aspiring

A lot of newer writers, and even many who've been writing for years, use the term "aspiring writer." I used to, too. It felt like a good compromise—I was still sharing that I enjoyed writing but wasn't claiming to actually *be* a writer.

Then I took a workshop with a literary agent who told us, point blank: "Go take 'aspiring' off your bio. You're here. You're doing the work. You're writers."

That advice stuck, and now I pass it on to every writer I work with.

Adding "aspiring" may feel small and inconsequential, but it's not. It reinforces the belief that you're not quite there yet, that you haven't earned the title. Every time you call yourself an aspiring writer, you're feeding the imposter syndrome that keeps you stuck.

So, I know you might be reading this and thinking that I'm being dramatic in telling you to immediately go to any social media presence you might have and change any mention of aspiring writer to simply say "writer"—I know this because I was once in your exact shoes—but I promise you this is bigger than just a disagreement over an adjective. It's a mindset shift. Making the conscious effort to start thinking about yourself as a writer rather than an aspiring one is the first step toward shattering your self-limiting beliefs so you can finally become the writer you dream of being.

3

WHY THIS STORY?

W<small>HEN</small> I <small>WORK WITH A NEW WRITER FOR COACHING,</small> I always begin by asking about their writing journey so far. Often, because they've come to me for help, this journey involves a series of starts and stops: stretches of being committed to their writing followed by longer periods where they can't seem to find the time or energy to put words on the page. Sometimes, they ping-pong between writing no matter what and feeling defeated and unable to keep going.

Once I understand their history, we shift toward the present goal—the story they've come to me to help them finish. After they share their story idea, I ask them a key question: *Why do you want to write this particular story?*

Sometimes, a client can answer right away. When there's a personal connection to the story's subject, it's often easier to articulate. But other times, there's a pause while they consider the question. For some, they'd never given it too much thought. They may say simply, "Because it seems like a good story," but I always encourage them to dig deeper.

Because without knowing *why* you're writing a story, finishing it can be incredibly difficult. Without a sense of why this particular story matters to you, you're more likely to switch to a new idea—or worse, give up on writing altogether—when you hit the tougher stretches of the process. Knowing your why can help you keep going, even on the days when that feels impossible.

Why You Need a Why

Some clients push back when I press them to identify their why. And I get it—most writers want to get to the writing. But writing a novel isn't a quick task. It takes time, energy, and commitment to bring a story from idea to finished manuscript. Taking a little time up front to understand what's driving you to tell this story is time well spent.

Since writing a novel is such a long process, it's almost guaranteed that you'll hit moments where you feel like giving up, where you question if you should find a new hobby, one that doesn't make you want to pull your hair out. That's when your why becomes essential. When you know why this story is important to you, you can return to that reason to motivate you when things get hard.

If you haven't taken the time to define why this story matters, what will carry you through when a major plot hole throws everything off track? Or when a critique partner points out areas that need heavy revision? What will motivate you to keep going instead of quitting? Even if you're determined to write a novel, if you don't know why *this* story matters, what's to stop you from hopping from one idea to the next, convinced the next one will be easier?

Most story ideas don't arrive perfectly outlined in our minds. First drafts are never perfect. Sticking with a story through drafts, critiques, and revisions takes a deep belief that *this story matters* and that making it the best it can be is worth the effort. You *can* sit down and write any story that pops into your head. But if the story doesn't mean something to you, sustaining the motivation to finish will be much harder than if you chose one that truly resonates.

And beyond motivation, knowing your why also deepens your storytelling. It creates a stronger connection between you and your characters, and therefore between your readers and the story. A story might sound good and include all the right ingredients to be a bestseller, but if the writer doesn't understand why they care about it, the reader won't either. A skilled writer can write a story that seemingly is well constructed—the plot works, the character arcs are in place, the setting is descriptive—but if the *emotional connection* isn't there, the story will likely fall flat.

Where does that connection come from? Your own investment in the story and their characters.

If you treat your characters like plot devices, readers will notice. If you can't articulate why you care about them, you won't be able to convey deep emotion on the page. And when stories fall flat, readers tend to move on.

It starts with you. To hook your readers and give them a story they care about, you have to care first.

Why Only You Can Write This Book

In writing groups, I often see writers worrying that their idea has already been taken. They're working on a project when they come across a book with a similar concept, and suddenly they feel like they can't continue.

But here's the truth: there are no original story ideas, only original perspectives.

When we look at story premises on a broad scale, many are

similar. What makes each story unique is the *lens* through which it's told.

Think about how many books you've read where the main character leaves their small hometown for the big city, only to return home and reconnect with someone from their past. Often, there's some kind of romantic element. And often, the character ends up realizing big city life isn't all they'd dream of and moves back to the small town.

We've all seen this premise over and over. And yet, we keep reading these books. Why? Because each author brings something new. A unique perspective. Different details. A fresh take.

This is why I always tell writers: *You are the only one who can write your story the way you envision it.* I could give the same premise to twenty writers, and I would get twenty different stories. Would there be some similarities? Of course. But each one would have its own voice and its own ideal reader.

While there's no shortage of books these days, there's also no shortage of readers craving a good story that speaks to them.

It's normal to wonder if your story matters, especially when the writing gets hard. You might think, *"What's the point? Couldn't someone else write this?"* But no one else can write it like *you*. No one else has your exact blend of life experiences, insights, and voice.

So, when writing feels difficult—and it will—remember this: you're the only one who can bring your story to life the way you imagine it. Keep going!

How To Identify Your Why

Some writers know their why immediately. Others have no idea. Some start with a clear message or experience they want to share; others begin with a story idea and only later realize what it means to them.

Rather than skipping over the question and diving into your draft, I encourage you to spend time exploring your why. Here are a few questions I often use with my coaching clients to get their brains turning. Consider journaling your answers to explore your thoughts more deeply.

- What about this story intrigued me initially?
- Did the idea come fully formed, or did I expand on a broader premise? What was the original idea, and why did I feel drawn to develop it?
- Who is the main character, and why do I feel compelled to share their story?
- What part of my own experience or emotions does this story reflect?
- What themes or messages am I trying to explore? Why do they matter to me?
- What do I hope readers take away from this story?

Why Your Why Needs to Be Bigger Than Money

I want to end this chapter by addressing the question many new writers have: can writers actually make a living from their writing?

Unfortunately, it's not a simple yes or no. The reality is that most writers don't earn enough to fully support themselves. However, many writers—both traditionally and indie published —*do* earn good money from writing.

But it's almost never from just one book.

Writers who earn a living exclusively from writing typically have multiple books under their belts. The more you publish, the more income opportunities you create. So, while it's abso-lutely possible to make good money from writing, if replacing your day job income is your *main* reason for writing a book, I urge you to either dig deeper for another motivator or channel your energy elsewhere.

Here's why: making good money from writing requires a lot of time, energy, perseverance, and dedication (and to an extent, luck and good timing). This is not as simple as writing one great book and then retiring to write in a cabin for the rest of your life. Chances are, you'll need to write multiple books to see any substantial financial gain, and even after several books, you still may not be making enough money to fully support yourself. If financial success is your only motivation, you're more likely to burn out or give up.

But if financial gain is a secondary goal—if you're driven by a love of storytelling, a need to express something meaningful, or a desire to connect with readers—then you're far more likely to stick with it. And that persistence is what often leads to eventual financial success.

Making money from your writing is a valid and worthwhile goal. You *deserve* to be paid for your work. But if money is the only thing driving you, you'll probably run out of steam long before you reach your goal. If instead, you keep showing up because you love writing and can't imagine *not* doing it, then you're on a path that can sustain you—and your readers—for years to come.

WHILE IT CAN BE TEMPTING to dive straight into drafting, I encourage you to pause and reflect on why this particular story matters to you. What draws you to it? Why now? Understanding the deeper reason you feel called to tell this story—and what's at stake if you walk away—will give you something powerful to hold onto when the writing gets hard. That clarity becomes your anchor, helping you stay the course when doubt creeps in or motivation fades.

4

DOES WRITING HAVE TO BE USEFUL TO BE WORTHWHILE?

A WHILE BACK, A FRIEND SHARED WITH ME THAT SHE WAS struggling to come up with a hobby for herself that was useful. When I asked her what she meant, she said she wanted something she could do to unwind and relax, but she couldn't think of anything useful enough to justify the time spent on it.

This immediately raised a red flag for me. Isn't the whole point of a hobby to disconnect from the constant need to be productive? In trying to find a hobby that was productive, I worried my friend was getting sucked even deeper into the very hustle culture she was trying to escape by picking up a new hobby.

Naturally, after this conversation, my mind went to writing and how this same mindset so often holds writers back from working toward their dream of writing a book.

So...does writing need to be "useful" to be worth our time and energy? Let's explore.

What Makes Something Useful?

Before we can dive into discussing whether writing needs to be useful to be worthwhile, we first need to consider what "useful" even means. That will shape how we apply the idea to writing.

The problem is, "useful" is a deeply subjective term. What one person finds useful, another might not. And even for the same person, what feels useful today might not feel useful a year from now.

The dictionary defines useful as "of a valuable or productive kind."[i] But our society often equates valuable and productive with monetizable. We're living in the age of hustle culture where the message is loud and clear: we should always be working toward something, even in our downtime.

There's a meme on social media where someone says they need to take a break, then immediately wonders whether there's a more productive way to take that break. This perfectly sums up the culture we live in. Even when we're trying to relax, we're being told that time must still be useful. We should be reading personal development books, building side businesses, or looking up Pinterest crafts for our kids. We've internalized the belief that every spare moment must either make us money or move us toward self-actualization.

No wonder my friend jumped straight to finding a hobby that was useful. If she did something purely for the joy of it, she'd feel like she was going against everything society has told her about how she should spend her time.

But what if I told you that something can be useful without making you rich or leading to some great epiphany?

If something brings you joy, its usefulness lies in exactly that —it brings you joy.

If something allows you to clear your mind and relax so you can wake up the next day with a clearer head and a sense of peace, then I'd argue it's useful even if it doesn't feel *productive* in the moment.

Taking a step back to examine what useful really means helps us see that useful and productive are not necessarily the same, no matter how often society tries to conflate the two. And while most of us hope that our writing may someday lead to publishing and financial compensation, I firmly believe that even if we never recoup the money we invest into our writing, even if we write solely for ourselves, and even if we never end up on the New York Times Bestseller list, if writing brings us any amount of joy, peace, or healing, then it is worth the time we invest into it.

But I think what my friend really meant when she said she wanted a hobby that was useful, and what many of the writers mean when they wrestle with this idea, is: *Will other people see this as a good use of my time?*

The issue with this way of thinking is that if we're constantly seeking external validation for how we spend our time, we'll always be chasing approval that may never come. And we'll likely end up unhappy with our choices.

The entire point of finding a hobby or writing a book should be to find something that fulfills *you*. If it doesn't do that, even if other people think it's useful, then it's not really serving you. And chances are, you'll just end up needing another hobby to escape from the first one.

It's a vicious cycle.

Breaking Away from Hustle Culture

The idea that we need to be productive *all the time* has become so deeply ingrained that many of us accept it without question. It's become a culture-wide limiting belief.

We're taught early on that to get a good job, we need to get into a good college and get good grades. To get ahead at work, we need to stay busy and prove our worth. And even in our free time, we're told to do something to improve our quality of life in some way. It's been hammered into our heads that if we're not striving, we're falling behind.

And this mindset can have severely damaging effects.

The COVID-19 pandemic allowed many of us to pause and reevaluate this mentality. But as life resumed its usual pace and the financial pressure of rising costs hit, we've largely given back into the concept of hustling.

I see this often with people who enjoy crafty hobbies—Cricut projects, sewing, crocheting, etc. The moment they mention their hobby, someone inevitably says, "Oh, you should start an Etsy shop! You could make so much money!"

But here's the thing: maybe they *could* make good money doing that. But maybe turning their hobby into a business would drain all the joy from it. Maybe it's not the right move for them. And that's okay.

Just because they choose not to monetize their creativity doesn't make it less valuable.

And the same goes for writing.

While most writers hope to publish, it takes a fair amount of time to create strong enough stories. Many writers have entire manuscripts sitting in literal or proverbial drawers that will never be seen by anyone else. Were those hours wasted? I would argue not.

Without the lessons learned from those manuscripts, they couldn't have become the writer they are now. And if you're just starting out writing, please know there's no way to get better without practicing writing. The more you write, the better you will be, and the better you are, the likelier you are to create a book you feel confident publishing. But even if no one ever reads that story, it mattered. It was an investment in your writing career and an investment in yourself.

This also holds true for writers who may not have any desire to publish. For some, writing is a personal thing they are doing solely for themselves. Writing can be a source of healing, joy, clarity, and creativity. That alone makes it worthwhile.

We could spend an entire book discussing the effects of hustle culture, but for our purposes, I just want you to see how easily it seeps into your thinking—especially when you're trying to decide whether writing a book is a good use of your time. If your default lens is "will this make me money?" you may be asking the wrong question.

Here's the thing I want you to take away from this: the factor that makes something worthwhile isn't money.

Most of us didn't start writing because we thought we'd get rich. We started because writing *gives* us something. And that something is your why. That's what makes your writing worthwhile.

It may take some (or a lot) of practice to shift away from evaluating everything in terms of productivity or profit. But the more you catch yourself doing it, and the more intentionally you question whether that way of thinking is serving you, the more natural it becomes to shift your focus.

What Does Success Mean to You?

If success isn't necessarily "making lots of money," then what *does* it look like?

Here's the thing: *you* get to decide. Success is subjective, and it means something different to everyone.

This is where many writers struggle. They've dreamed of writing a book their whole lives, but somewhere along the way, they absorbed the belief that writing a book didn't equal success.

So, they chase other things society says will make them success-ful, only to find they're miserable. By denying themselves the opportunity to write, they're denying themselves the opportunity to be happy.

This is a theme I see often with my coaching clients, and it's a theme I've lived myself.

To be fair, we all need to earn a living. That's just the reality of the world we live in, and if we try to pretend that's not true, we'll quickly learn that was incredibly naïve. But not everything we do needs to turn a profit. Just because you work a full-time job doesn't mean you can't also write a book.

When I think about this, I think about my son and the hopes I have for his future. My biggest hope for him in life is that he is happy—truly, unabashedly, genuinely happy. Sure, I hope he's financially secure. But my goal is to raise a son who grows up to chase a life that brings him joy, even if that looks different than whatever I might envision for him. If he can come to me later in life and say "Mom, I'm truly happy with my life and wouldn't change a thing," then I'll feel like he's successful.

And if I want that for him, then I owe it to him and to myself to want the same for me.

If writing is what brings me happiness, then being a writer is my version of success.

It can be hard to untangle our own definition of success from the one society hands us. But doing that inner work and defining success for yourself is crucial.

Maybe your version of success isn't about money at all. Maybe it's about seeing your name on a book cover. Or creating stories that touch people. Or simply enjoying the act of writing. But until you name *your* version of success and start making decisions in alignment with it, you'll always feel a disconnect, even if you're technically succeeding by society's standards.

When I work with coaching clients, one of the first questions I ask is: *what's your definition of success?*

Often, they repeat back beliefs they've been conditioned to hold, or they don't have a clear answer. In those cases, I ask them to journal through it. And I'm going to ask you to do the same.

Even if you think you know what success means to you, it's powerful to write it down. Putting your definition on paper can help clarify what matters most and where your energy should go.

And if your current daily life isn't aligned with your personal definition of success, ask yourself why. What changes (big or small) could you make to better align your life with what success really means to *you?*

———————

THE HUSTLE CULTURE mentality can be difficult to break away from, but gaining clarity around your own definitions of success and usefulness can help guide your decisions about how you spend your time. Remember that useful doesn't have to mean productive in the traditional sense, and success isn't limited to financial gain. If writing brings you joy, meaning, or a sense of purpose, that alone makes it worthwhile—regardless of what the world says. Your time and creativity don't need to justify themselves to anyone but you.

5

WHAT ARE SELF-LIMITING BELIEFS?

WHEN I STARTED MY BOOK COACHING BUSINESS, I KNEW that I wanted to do more than just help writers draft their novels. In the writing communities I was part of, I saw a lot of writers saying they were stuck, but reading between the lines, it was clear their challenges often weren't with the writing itself. More often, they were struggling with something deeper—some form of self-limiting belief that was preventing them from writing.

With my background in mental health counseling, I recognized that many of the obstacles these writers were facing went beyond typical writing woes. But when a writer shares in a group that they're having trouble focusing, they're often met with surface-level advice to address the apparent issue: set a timer and do writing sprints, change your location, wake up before the kids. These are all great tips, but if the root issue is a self-limiting belief, such as imposter syndrome or a fear of failure, those strategies alone aren't going to fully resolve the problem.

The self-limiting beliefs that prevent us from writing may be specific to writing, but often they're more pervasive than that. These are often beliefs we hold about ourselves or the world that spill over into our writing lives. And since these beliefs are so deeply ingrained, overcoming them takes intentional effort.

In my research for this book, I came across a quote by Nobel Peace Prize winner Wangari Maathai that perfectly articulated how self-limiting beliefs can interfere with our writing. She said, "We often preoccupy ourselves with the symptoms, whereas if we went to the root cause of the problems, we would be able to overcome the problems once and for all."[i] We so often get caught up in addressing the symptoms of our issues and spend a lot of time putting bandages over them. But if we don't make the effort to dig deep and explore what's at the heart of those symptoms, then no matter how many bandages we put in place, those root causes will continue to plague our writing lives.

In my work with coaching clients, I always keep an eye out for what's happening beneath the surface. If they're struggling to write, I want to understand what self-limiting beliefs might be at play. We work together to identify and challenge those beliefs throughout the writing process, and we stay alert for any new ones that may arise along the way. My goal is not just to help writers get words on the page, but to help them become confident, lifelong writers who proudly claim their identity as such.

So, let's look at some of the most common self-limiting beliefs that hold writers back—and how you can begin to move past them.

Imposter Syndrome

Imposter syndrome is a term that gets tossed around a lot in the writing community. It refers to when someone doubts their abilities despite evidence that they're capable and fears being exposed as a fraud.

Because writing doesn't require a formal degree or training, many writers feel uncertain about whether they "count" as writers, especially if they're not yet published. Unlike a career path like accounting, which often comes with degrees, certifications, and job titles, the writing path is much murkier. And while there are MFA degrees and formal trainings for writers, even those who complete these often struggle with imposter syndrome before they're published (and sometimes even after).

As we discussed in Chapter 2, there's often a mental image of what a "real writer" looks like, but this usually doesn't match the reality. Yes, there are full-time authors who earn a living from writing. But far more writers are squeezing their work into the margins of busy lives. Some write one book a year; others take a decade.

What surprised me as I became more involved in the writing world was how many traditionally published authors still struggle with imposter syndrome. Even after landing a book deal—the kind of validation many writers dream of—they continue to wrestle with self-doubt.

Even Maya Angelou struggled with imposter syndrome. She famously said, "I have written eleven books, but each time I think 'uh oh, they're going to find out now. I've run a game on everybody, and they're going to find me out."[ii] And if *Maya Angelou* wasn't immune from imposter syndrome, then really no one is.

The key to remember is this: imposter syndrome is not a reflection of your talent. It stems from faulty beliefs. These can include unrealistic standards, a fear of failure, or the idea that being competent means never doubting yourself. We tell ourselves that if we were really successful, we'd always feel confident—and when we don't, we assume that must mean we're faking it.

But our idea of what successful looks like is generally idealistic. Successful individuals don't feel successful every single day. Everyone has ups and downs, and everyone has internal beliefs that threaten their confidence. Imposter syndrome can feel so paralyzing because it attacks where we're weakest: it latches onto one small fragment of doubt and catastrophizes until we're certain we're frauds—even when there's evidence to the contrary—and we become terrified that others are going to call us out.

When imposter syndrome rears its ugly head, it's important to take a step back, acknowledge what you're feeling, and remember that it's normal. Even seasoned, multi-published authors experience it. Imposter syndrome can feel paralyzing, but naming it can take away some of its power.

When clients come to me struggling with imposter syndrome, I encourage them to write out their "credentials." By credentials, I don't just mean degrees or job titles, although these things could be included if the individual has them. But beyond those formal credentials, what real-life experience do they have that makes them qualified to write the story they want to write? What evidence supports the fact that they are competent writers?

For example, if a client comes to me wanting to write a story about the world of competitive gymnastics, if she was a competitive gymnast herself, that's a credential. Or perhaps a teacher once told her she was a strong writer, or she won a short story contest. All of that counts.

Create your list, and keep it somewhere you can refer back to when the doubt creeps in. And remember: imposter syndrome doesn't mean you're not a good writer. It just means you're human.

The Perfection Myth

Another self-limiting belief many writers struggle with is the idea that their draft needs to be perfect. While on a cognitive level, I think most writers understand that their first draft isn't meant to be perfect, having the courage to write the "shitty" first draft is challenging.

Spending a large chunk of our time working on a draft that is still going to require a lot of work can feel disheartening. Looking at a rough draft that falls short of our vision can shake our confidence and make us question if we really have the skills to write that story we're imagining after all. And so, writers spend hours staring at blank screens because they can't come up with the right words.

But the truth is, you often need to write the wrong words before you can find the right ones. Getting something on the page, even if it's not quite what you wanted to say, gives you material to shape. Editing a rough sentence is much easier than creating the perfect one out of nothing.

When I draft, I keep a Post-it on my computer that says, "Just write." I need that constant reminder, or my brain will keep shutting down and shifting over to scroll social media. Writing sentences that aren't yet perfect feels like a threat to my ego, and so I have to keep granting myself permission to just write and worry about fixing it later.

But perfectionism is often a mask for something deeper: fear. We *know* there's no such thing as a perfect book—after all, writing is an art, and there is no such thing as perfect in art. And yet, we chase perfection because it gives us an excuse not to finish.

If we never finish, we don't have to face criticism. We don't risk rejection. We don't have to move on to the next scary thing.

But if we never finish, we don't know the positive consequences that also await us. We don't get to experience the joy of seeing our work in the world. We don't get to hear from readers who loved our story. We don't give our loved ones the chance to celebrate our success. We don't get to write the next book.

While striving for perfection may seem like we're being diligent authors, it's usually a defense mechanism. But if we want to be published authors, we have to be brave enough to finish, even if the result isn't perfect.

The Lie of Not Having Enough Time

One of the most common reasons writers give for not writing is a lack of time. And to be fair, life is full. Between jobs, families, and everything else, finding time to write can feel impossible.

If only we had more time, we tell ourselves—we'd churn out story after story and be the successful bestselling authors we know we're meant to be.

But then come the moments when the universe calls us on our bluff. We're given a chunk of free time and gleefully sit down at our desk to write...only, the words don't come.

Instead of effortlessly writing our stories, we're paralyzed by the blank page. And then our thoughts begin spiraling: if we were *real* writers, the words would come; if we were *real* writers, this wouldn't be so difficult.

We let these thoughts take root in our mind, and then we question if we're simply not meant to be writers.

And then we stop writing.

The truth is, time isn't usually the real issue. Novels have been written on lunch hours, during baby nap times, and in the margin time in the mornings and evenings before and after the rest of the world is awake. Novels can and have been written by finding five minutes here and ten minutes there. Most often, time isn't what's *really* stopping us from writing our stories. It's usually something deeper.

In therapy, there's a concept called the "presenting issue." This is the reason someone gives for seeking help, but many times, this isn't the real issue that needs to be addressed. For writers, "not enough time" is often the presenting issue, but the true issue is often fear, perfectionism, or some other self-limiting belief. A lack of time is only a symptom. And if the underlying issue isn't addressed, then even when an individual carves out hours in their schedule to write, writing still won't happen.

To be clear, by no means am I saying here any form of "we all have the same 24 hours." This cliched advice ignores the reality that some of us simply have more going on than others, and while we all have 24 hours in a day, we don't all have an equal number of hours to devote to writing. As a mother to a preschooler, I don't have the same 24 hours I had before I became a parent. Even when my son is asleep or at school, my mental bandwidth isn't the same as it used to be—and that's okay.

This isn't about blaming yourself for not writing. It's about being honest. Is time really the problem? Or are you saying you don't have time because you're avoiding addressing a deeper issue?

Journaling can be a helpful tool here. To start, reflect on your belief that a lack of time has been preventing you from writing. Have you actually looked for time to write, or have you just assumed you have none because you feel so busy? Often, people who say they don't have time to write haven't actually sat down with their schedule to find it. They just feel overwhelmed and busy all day, every day, so it seems natural to assume there's no room left for writing.

But when we do sit down and examine our schedules, even if it's not long stretches of uninterrupted time, many people discover they *can* find small snippets. These pockets of time can add up to meaningful progress, even if they don't look like the ideal writing conditions we imagine.

If you *have* carved out time to write, what happened? Did you follow through? Or did something get in the way? If something prevented you from sitting down to write, consider whether it was truly unavoidable or if it was something you could have said no to. After all, there will always be things vying for our attention. It's up to us to set and protect the boundaries that keep our writing time sacred.

Of course, true emergencies and unexpected situations do arise, but more often, the things that steal our writing time are things we could have declined. In those situations, I encourage you to treat your writing time the same way you would a job. If you were scheduled to work on a Tuesday from 9 a.m. to 5 p.m. and someone asked you to go shopping, you'd probably say, "I'm sorry, I have to work that day." The same principle applies to your writing: "I'm sorry, I'm writing then." And if you *do* choose to use that time differently, try to *reschedule* your writing time rather than letting it vanish entirely.

If you did sit down to write but couldn't get any words down, the root issue likely isn't time. Pay attention to the thoughts running through your mind in those moments. Notice what you do instead—do you keep flipping over to social media? Do you call your mom? These thoughts and behaviors are clues that can point you toward the underlying mindset blocks that are actually keeping you from writing.

Fear of Failure

The last major self-limiting belief I want to talk about is the fear of failure. Being an author means putting ourselves out into the world in a way that feels incredibly vulnerable. For fiction writers especially, there's often a fear that people—especially those closest to us—will make assumptions about our lives, values, and beliefs based on what we write. And because publishing means that anyone can read our stories, there's an added layer of exposure. It can feel like strangers and loved ones alike are peering straight into our minds.

But just as we need to create our own definitions of success, we also need to define what failure means to us. Like success, failure is subjective. One person might see publishing a book that only sells three copies a failure, but someone else might view that as a huge success: they wrote a novel and had the courage to share it with the world. Like success, if we allow other people's definitions of failure to shape our choices, we risk living lives that don't feel authentic to who we are.

I'm sure you've heard this piece of advice before: "Doubt kills more dreams than failure ever will." I see this quote on social media all the time and, honestly, usually roll my eyes and scroll past. *I know, I know,* I tell myself. It doesn't mean failure sucks any less. But this quote is shared repeatedly for a reason. Many of us fear failure, but it's *doubt* that often stops us before we even try. And if we allow our self-doubts to hold us back, we'll end up looking back at a life full of "I wish I had's" instead of accomplishments we can take pride in. And that may sound cliched to the point of being exhausting, but it doesn't make it any less true.

It can feel terrifying to imagine putting your story into the world and being met with negative feedback. But I promise you that while a bad review is likely to hurt, it won't hurt as much as not seeing your dream through and always wondering if you could have done it. Don't let the fear of something that *might* happen keep you from taking the chance.

Spend some time exploring what failure means to *you*. Not to your parents, your partner, your old high school teacher, but to *you*. Then, ask yourself: what's the worst-case scenario if I fail? Of course, it never feels good to fail. But often with failure comes the opportunity to learn and improve.

Part of being a writer is accepting that criticism comes with the territory. Not every agent, publisher, or reader will love what you write. Some people just won't be your audience. But others might offer feedback that helps you become a stronger writer and moves you closer to your goals.

Failure is inevitable, but it doesn't have to be final. And when we stop seeing it as something to be feared and instead accept it as part of the process, it loses some of its power.

———

SELF-LIMITING BELIEFS CAN BE SNEAKY. They often disguise themselves as facts that we easily accept as truth. But these beliefs are often at the root of our writing struggles, and making an effort to uncover them is the first step toward a writing life that feels less like an uphill battle and more like a creative collaboration with ourselves. In the next chapter, we'll explore how to start shifting these beliefs so you can write with greater freedom, confidence, and joy.

6

OVERCOMING SELF-LIMITING BELIEFS

Now that we've explored self-limiting beliefs in depth and how they shape your writing struggles, let's turn our attention to how you can start shifting them.

Battling self-limiting beliefs isn't easy. It takes effort to identify them and even more effort to overcome them. Because these beliefs are often deeply ingrained in our thinking, it requires consistent practice to catch them when they surface and continue to work through them. But, as we discussed in the previous chapter, addressing these root causes will be far more effective in the long run than continuing to put bandages over the symptoms.

So, let's dig in.

Raise Awareness

The first step in overcoming self-limiting beliefs is to become aware of them. These thoughts are often automatic, and because we've accepted them as truth for so long, we no longer question their validity. For example, the belief that we don't have enough time to write is often seen as being a fact. But when we take the time to dig deeper, we may realize it's just a surface-level symptom of something bigger.

One of my favorite tools for raising awareness around self-limiting beliefs is the Miracle Question. This technique, used in counseling and coaching, helps clients envision the outcome they want and identify steps to get there. Though simple, it's a powerful way to uncover hidden self-limiting beliefs that might be holding a writer back.

The Miracle Question poses a simple question to the client:

Suppose tonight, while you sleep, a miracle happens and all your problems as a writer are solved—but you don't know the miracle occurred. What do you notice in the morning that tells you something is different?

Clients then reflect on this and describe how their writing life would feel or look.

It sounds incredibly simple, and in many ways, it is. But by focusing on what would be *different* rather than what's *wrong*, the Miracle Question bypasses negativity and resistance. Instead of asking, "Why can't you get any writing done?" we ask, "What would it look like if you consistently were?" That shift helps writers move into a solution-focused mindset.

When a writer shares their "miracle morning" with me, what they're really describing is what they *wish* they could do but can't currently—because something is stopping them.

And often, that something is a self-limiting belief.

If someone says they wake up and start writing without self-doubt, the underlying belief might be: *I'm not a good enough writer.*

If they say they've stopped comparing themselves to others,

the belief might be: *Everyone else is ahead of me and I'll never be as good.*

If they say they can introduce themselves as a writer without feeling like a fraud, they may believe: *I'm not a real writer.*

By examining what would be different in your miracle morning, you can more clearly see what beliefs are holding you back.

And once you've spotted a self-limiting belief, you can begin questioning its validity.

Reframe Your Thoughts

One of my favorite interventions from my counseling training is the reframe. Reframing is when you take a negative thought and shift your perspective around it so it becomes more positive. This isn't about ignoring reality or pretending everything is fine when it isn't. It's about challenging thoughts that are unhelpful and intentionally viewing them through a different lens.

When you notice a belief that feels discouraging, pause and ask yourself: *Is this thought absolutely true? Where did it come from? Is there another, kinder way to look at this?*

Here are a few examples of powerful reframes:

- "I'm not a real writer" becomes "I am a writer because I write."
- "I don't have time to write" becomes "Even small segments of time can add up to big results."
- "I'm not a good enough writer to write a book" becomes "I become a better writer by writing."

See how these shifts present a different way of looking at the same thought? Reframing isn't about toxic positivity or forcing yourself to magically feel more confident. It's about subtly and continuously working to change your mindset so that, over time, these thoughts will more likely be the automatic ones that come to your mind over the negative ones. It's about recognizing that you're not beholden to these negative thoughts. *You* have the power to change them—you just have to choose to do so.

Add the "Yet"

A while back, I read *Girl, Stop Apologizing* by Rachel Hollis, and something she said really clicked with me. She said, "Your inexperience doesn't mean you won't succeed; it means you haven't yet."[i] This simple reframe takes almost no effort, but it overwhelmingly changes a negative thought to more positive, hopeful one.

And of course, I immediately began thinking about how this can be applied to writing.

Just because you haven't written a book *yet*, doesn't mean you can't.

When self-limiting beliefs make you doubt your ability to write a novel, try adding "yet" to the end of the sentence.

If your self-limiting belief is, "I can't write this story because I don't know enough about the French revolution," it now becomes, "I can't write this story because I don't know enough about the French revolution...yet."

That one little word shifts everything. It turns your negative, self-limiting thought into a statement that gives you complete control. Okay, you don't know enough about the French revolution to write a specific story you have in mind. That's fine. How can you learn more? Not only is the sentence more positive, it also naturally gives way to brainstorming action steps.

I truly believe nothing is out of reach if we're willing to put in the time, energy, and effort. So, next time you're faced with a belief that feels final, try adding "yet" and see what doors it opens.

Find the Evidence

Another cognitive-behavioral technique I often use with my coaching clients is the concept of *show me the evidence*.

The idea behind this is that when someone makes a negative claim about themselves, we ask them to back it up. This is especially helpful when trying to dismantle self-limiting beliefs because, more often than not, there's little (if any) real evidence supporting them.

For example, if a writer tells me they're not a real writer because they work a day job, I'll point out that most writers don't make a living from their writing, especially not at first.

If they say, "But I haven't published anything," I'll remind them that no one starts out published. They have to write something first.

When doing this yourself, ask: is this belief really true 100% of the time? Are there exceptions?

Even identifying one exception begins to weaken the belief. Suddenly, it's no longer an all-or-nothing truth.

Next, examine the "evidence" you've been using to support this belief. Is there faulty logic buried within it? Is it a misinterpretation your mind created to justify a fear?

By breaking down the "proof" behind our self-limiting beliefs, we can begin to loosen their grip on us.

Positive Affirmations

Positive affirmations are short, intentional phrases we repeat to ourselves to retrain our brain. Once you've identified your self-limiting beliefs, you can create affirmations that directly counter them. With practice, these affirmations can become the new automatic thoughts that arise when you sit down to write.

For example, if your belief is *I'm not a real writer*, your positive affirmation might be *I am a real writer*.

Again, this sounds simple—but that doesn't mean it's easy. We can't retrain our brains overnight. Repetition and consistency are key. The more you catch the self-limiting belief when it arises, challenge it, and replace it with a more empowering one, the more your brain will begin to adopt that new pattern.

Over time, the old belief loses its power, and the new one takes root.

To help you get started, I've created a set of free printable affirmation cards featuring powerful, writer-specific phrases designed to counter common self-limiting beliefs. You can post them near your writing space, keep them in your notebook, or use them as daily reminders of your creative strength. Just sign up for my email list at www.lisafellinger.com/affirmation-card-deck to download your set and keep these supportive messages close at hand.

OVERCOMING SELF-LIMITING beliefs won't happen overnight, but every small step chips away at the walls that have kept you stuck. By raising your awareness, challenging your thoughts, and actively reshaping your inner narrative, you're reclaiming your power as a writer.

While the techniques outlined here might seem incredibly

simple, it takes a conscious effort to become aware of these thoughts and continually work to counter them. And while these beliefs may not vanish completely, with time, practice, and compassion, their hold will loosen. And in their place, you'll begin to build a mindset rooted in growth, confidence, and possibility.

Keep showing up. Keep doing the work. And remember: the only thing standing between you and your dream writing life is a belief—and beliefs can change.

7

WHY DO WE PROCRASTINATE?

PROCRASTINATION IS SOMETHING I STRUGGLE WITH regularly. It's not uncommon for a task to get bumped from one day or week to the next in my planner, until ultimately, I'm left with no choice but to do it because it's due in...four hours. But most of the time, once I finally do sit down and focus, the task doesn't take nearly as long as I feared, and it's rarely as hard as I'd built it up to be in my mind.

Writing this book, for example, has been on my to-do list for a while, but week after week, it sat unfinished while everything else (or almost everything else) got checked off. But now that I've carved out time for it and am forcing myself to sit down and get words on the page, it hasn't been as difficult as I imagined. In fact, more often than not, it's been fun.

So, why do we procrastinate? Contrary to what we might believe, procrastination doesn't come from laziness or a lack of motivation. Instead, it's a response to fear and discomfort around doing something new or challenging. When a task feels difficult, it can feel like a threat to our sense of competence. So, to protect ourselves, we avoid it.

But as anyone who procrastinates knows, avoidance only

causes the task to weigh more heavily on us. We know the task still needs to get done. We know it's unlikely to get easier if we keep waiting. Yet it's hard to make ourselves sit down and do something that risks making us feel inadequate—so, we wait until we're up against a deadline and no longer have a choice.

The problem is, when it comes to writing, we usually don't have a hard deadline. Unless you're already under contract with a publisher, no one is standing over your shoulder telling you it's time to write. And without that external pressure, many books sit unfinished or never get started. We keep saying we'll write next week, next month, next year...until years go by and we're still without a finished manuscript.

So, what's really behind our procrastination? Let's take a closer look at what might be fueling your avoidance and how it connects to deeper beliefs and fears.

Fear of Failure

Many writers carry a deep fear of failure. It's no secret that writing a book is challenging. After all, if it were easy, far more people would do it. But beyond the challenge itself, there's the vulnerability that comes with trying. Putting our dreams out there and risking disappointment is scary. We worry that people will judge us or laugh at us if we say we want to write a book and then never get published. We worry we'll send out queries only to be rejected again and again. We worry we'll revise for the fifth time and still hear, "It's not quite there yet." We fear that the hard work won't pay off.

But rejection and criticism are part of the writing journey. If we want to grow as writers, we need feedback. If your goal is traditional publishing, rejections from agents or publishers are inevitable. After all, they receive more submissions than they can possibly accept. Even if you plan to self-publish, someone out there won't connect with your story, and they might leave a public review saying so.

It's crucial to remember that none of that is a reflection of who you are as a writer or a person. Failure is only failure if it stops you from writing. If you receive feedback that your story needs more work, you have a choice. You can stop there, or you can see it as an opportunity to grow, to strengthen your story and become a better writer. If you get a bad review, you can spiral—or you can look at the twenty other readers who loved it and remember that no book is for everyone. If a review offers something helpful, you might take that into account. But if it's simply a mismatch in taste, let it go.

Holding yourself back because you're afraid of failing means you'll never know what you're capable of. Fear is powerful. But letting fear decide for you keeps you from reaching your potential. If writing is something that matters to you—if it's something you can't imagine *not* doing—then you owe it to yourself to swallow that fear, sit down at your keyboard, and write the words.

It's okay to be afraid. But sometimes, we just have to write scared. Force the fear aside and put in the work. Trust the process and know that messy drafts are part of the journey and with each revision, you're getting closer to the story you envision.

Yes, writing when you're afraid of failure is scary. But I promise it's not as scary as never realizing your potential, never chasing your dream, because you let fear win.

Write the story. Keep showing up for your dreams. You don't want to look back one day and wonder if you could have done it if only you hadn't been afraid.

Fear of Success

On the opposite end of the spectrum is the fear of success. I know—that sounds like it can't possibly be real. But many writers struggle with it, whether they realize it or not.

Fear of success isn't exactly fearing the success itself, but the change it might bring. Humans are creatures of habit. Just as failure shifts our sense of identity, so does success. And that shift can feel just as scary. Sometimes, to avoid change, we sabotage ourselves—consciously or unconsciously.

If you succeed in writing and publishing a book, your life changes. You're no longer "working on a book." You're an author, and that comes with new responsibilities: marketing, deadlines, maybe a book tour. Writing becomes a career, not just a creative outlet. And that change can feel intimidating.

Writers might also fear success because of how it could affect their relationships. If you're the first in your writing group to publish, you might worry others will view you differently. You might worry they'll treat you with jealousy or resentment. They might assume you think you're "better than them" now. But here's the truth: while you can't control how others will react, you *can* control how *you* react. If you keep showing up with humility and support, any tension that might arise isn't your responsibility to fix. Your success may stir something in someone else, but that's their work to do, not yours.

Others may fear backlash for publishing. Maybe your story includes themes your family might disapprove of. Maybe you're uncomfortable with the idea of marketing and worry about how people will perceive your self-promotion. That fear of being visible, or being judged, can keep writers from finishing their books. But again, others' reactions are not your responsibility. Those are their issues to address.

Fear of success is hard to spot because it often hides behind reasonable-sounding excuses. We say we don't have time, when really, we're avoiding the discomfort of what comes next. But if you suspect fear of success might be holding you back, take a closer look. Is it truly a time issue, or is it that voice inside saying, *"This is too big, too scary."*

Succeeding at anything comes with uncertainty. That's what makes it meaningful. Change is hard, even when it's positive. But standing still out of fear won't feel good in the long run.

Do the work. Ask the hard questions. But *please*—don't let fear of change stop you from achieving something that matters deeply to you. You owe it to yourself to see it through.

It Doesn't Have to Be Perfect, You Just Have to Start

Procrastination and perfectionism tend to go hand-in-hand. Often, we put off writing because we're afraid what we write won't be good enough. We stare at the blank page, wanting the perfect words to appear, and when they don't, we find other things to do—scrolling, organizing, cleaning. Literally anything to avoid the discomfort of writing imperfect words.

I know it feels scary to write something that isn't perfect, but perfect doesn't exist in writing. It especially doesn't exist in first drafts. Writing is a process of multiple drafts for a reason. There's so much effort behind what eventually reads as effortless. The first draft is where the mess happens, where you get to explore and play and figure things out. Instead of fearing that, lean into it. Give yourself permission to write the messy first draft.

I might be the odd writer out, but I personally prefer revision over drafting. Once I have something on the page, I can work with it. Staring at a blank screen feels overwhelming. But like Jodi Picoult said, "I may write garbage, but you can always edit garbage. You can't edit a blank page."[i] A rough draft doesn't mean you're not good at writing. It means you're writing. This is the process. Even bestselling authors start with clunky sentences and awkward scenes.

But as much as I love revision, I have to get through the drafting stage in order to revise. I've had to train myself to just *get the words down*. I still hate facing the blank page, and yes, I still procrastinate. But when I remind myself this is just a draft —that it will get better with revision—I'm more able to write freely. I silence my inner editor and focus on making progress, not perfection.

That first draft doesn't need to be perfect. It just needs to exist. You can't revise words that aren't written. So, trust the process and get the words down. You'll fix them later. But first, you have to start.

8

OVERCOME WRITER'S BLOCK FOR GOOD

WRITER'S BLOCK IS THE ARCHENEMY OF WRITERS. SITTING down at the computer, thinking we're ready to write but the words just *won't come* is one of the most frustrating experiences a writer can have. I know of writers who have lost years of writing time to writer's block, and countless others who have at least lost days here and there over this frustration. But what exactly is writer's block, and how can you overcome it? Let's take a look.

Is Writer's Block Real?

Writer's block describes the predicament when a writer feels like they have the time, energy, and space to work, but when they sit down to actually write, nothing happens. They stare at the blank screen or page, but ultimately, they walk away with little to nothing written.

It's incredibly frustrating for writers because, on the surface, everything they need is in place: they've set aside the time, minimized distractions, and know the story they're working on—but still, the words won't come.

There's a bit of a disagreement in the writing community about whether writer's block is "real." Some argue that it's simply self-sabotage and the writer just needs to work harder at finding the words. While this advice might work for small bouts of writer's block where a writer struggles for a day or two, for those who are confronted with debilitating, discouraging stretches where they can't get any writing done, "work harder" feels like a misguided suggestion that invalidates their experience. They *are* working hard; it's just not working.

What often gets lost in translation when writers debate whether writer's block is real is their definition of "real." Writer's block is absolutely real in the sense that something is blocking a writer from producing words despite their best efforts. But is there some divine force playing mind games with us? No.

Writer's block is simply self-limiting beliefs getting in our way—often operating so subconsciously that we don't even realize they're there. On the surface, everything looks fine, and we can't identify any obvious sabotaging thoughts. But when we dig deeper, writer's block generally traces back to some form of limiting belief.

The good news? Since the source of writer's block is internal, we have control over it. While it's not easy, putting in the work to uncover and resolve the underlying issues can free us from its grasp.

Easy? No.

Worth it? Absolutely.

How Self-Limiting Beliefs Create Writer's Block

As we talked about in previous chapters, self-limiting beliefs are the ideas we hold about ourselves or the world that prevent us from writing. Sometimes it's obvious how these beliefs sabotage our efforts. But often, it's not clear what beliefs are at play or how they're interfering. And when nothing obvious comes to mind, we default to calling our struggle "writer's block," assuming we have no control over it.

But when we're feeling blocked—when we feel like we have everything we need to write but still can't make progress—it's time to take a hard look at the thoughts showing up during our writing time.

Journaling can be a powerful way to get to the root of these hidden thought patterns. Try journaling about your feelings toward writing and being a writer. Pay close attention to what thoughts arise when you actually sit down to write and write them down without judgment. You might also want to revisit the Miracle Question exercise discussed in Chapter 6.

If journaling on your own doesn't reveal the root of your writer's block, working with a book coach or a therapist can help. As a book coach, when my clients struggle to make progress despite setting aside writing time, we explore their thought patterns together, searching for self-limiting beliefs that may be interfering. Since these beliefs often feel like absolute truths to us, it's much easier for a third party to spot them—just like it's easier for someone else to spot issues in our manuscripts that we can't see ourselves.

When you're too close to something, it's hard to see it clearly.

The Case for Rest

Another major contributor to writer's block is burnout. As discussed earlier, we live in a very "hustle" oriented world. We're constantly bombarded with images of others' progress, advice on how to be more productive, and the not-so-subtle message that downtime is for the lazy.

But hustling every day will eventually end only one way: burnout.

Striving for big goals is wonderful. But if we never give ourselves a chance to breathe, clear our minds, and recharge, we'll eventually burn out.

I recently read that our culture doesn't really practice self-care; we practice "after-care" instead. We recognize the importance of taking a break, but only once things have gotten so bad that we can't function anymore. And we pretend that this is self-care.

But self-care is meant to be preventative. It means setting aside intentional time to rest *before* we become burnt-out disasters.

And I get it. With piles of laundry, dishes, deadlines, mouths to feed, groceries to buy, and limited writing time, it's easy to fall into the trap of thinking we must spend every free moment working on our goals. That every spare minute must go toward writing.

But that mindset only leads to burnout—and burnout feeds writer's block.

Ultimately, taking time for true self-care will make you *more* productive in the long run.

When we allow ourselves to truly rest—to step away from all the demands—we come back to our goals with clearer minds and more motivation to continue. We come back with energy that we just don't have when we're constantly forcing ourselves to keep going in the name of "being productive."

I encourage you to start shifting your mindset around productivity. Sometimes, the best thing you can do for your writing is to step away for a bit, trusting that when you return, you'll be better equipped to actually make progress.

Consider scheduling regular self-care rather than waiting until you're completely overwhelmed and defeated. Not only do you deserve it, but it will pay off ten-fold by helping you avoid burnout and writer's block.

Reconnect with Your Why

Remember that "why" we identified back in Chapter 3? This is exactly why we did that exercise.

Your why is the driving force behind your desire to write a novel. It's the reason the writing life called to you in the first place—and the reason you decided it was worth investing your time and energy.

But sometimes, in the chaos of daily life or situational circumstances, we lose sight of our why. We start to wonder: *Why am I doing this? Is it even worth it?*

That's why I encouraged you to write your why down someplace you'll see it often. So that even on the days where writing feels impossible and you question if it's worth the effort, you have that reminder staring you in the face.

If you're struggling with writer's block, if you feel like the energy you're pouring into writing no longer feels worth it, go back and read your why. It may not solve the block immediately, but reconnecting with your motivation can fuel you to work through the issue causing it.

Give Yourself Permission to Quit

I've said it before, and I'll say it again: writing a novel is hard.

There's no way to sugarcoat that. If you want to write a novel that resonates with readers, it's going to require hard work. From writing the words, to revising the words and revising them again, to learning about the craft of writing and publishing, writing a novel is never a get-rich-quick scheme.

And when writing gets really hard, it's natural to wonder how much easier life would be if we just...stopped.

And that's a fair question. After all, no one is forcing us to write. If you're early on in your writing journey, chances are no one would even know if you quit since they may not have even known you started.

It might seem counterintuitive, but when I hit my hardest writing days, I remind myself that it's okay to walk away if I want to. I've closed my computer on multiple occasions and told myself I might not come back to it.

Why? Because giving myself permission to quit takes the pressure off and allows me a chance to pause and catch my breath. It reminds me that *I'm* the one choosing this path, and if writing no longer brings me joy, it's okay to stop.

But every single time, I argue myself back out of quitting. Once the pressure is removed, once I've reminded myself that *I'm* the one who wants this, and once I consider what life without writing would look like, the thought of quitting seems absurd.

Yes, life might be harder than it needs to be sometimes because of my desire to write and publish books. Sure, it looks like it would be a lot easier to relax every evening by watching television and *not* having to think about my writing. But would I be happy with that decision? That's a question only you can answer for yourself, but for me, it's a resounding no.

If you're struggling with writer's block or a season of life where writing feels especially challenging, take the pressure off. Remind yourself that you can quit if you want to. No disaster will occur.

But my suspicion is if you're reading this book, you'll realize —just like I do every time—that writing brings meaning to your life.

And then you'll open your manuscript back up and keep chugging along.

9

FINDING TIME TO WRITE

FINDING TIME TO WRITE WHEN LIFE IS CHAOTIC CAN FEEL overwhelming and like a lost cause. But if you don't make the time to write when you're busy, you likely won't find it when you're *not* busy either.

Someone said this to me a while back, and at first, I rebelled against it. What did they mean by that? Of course I'd have more time to write once life calmed down. I just needed to get through this rough patch, but then in a couple of months everything would slow down, and I'd have plenty of time to work on my writing.

But here's the thing: inevitably, just as one part of life winds down, something else crops up in its place. It's rare for life to be entirely calm and free of obligations. And yes, there will be seasons when we have more time to dedicate to writing than others. But the point is, if you don't prioritize your writing when life is busy, you probably won't prioritize it when life gets easier, either.

When I really thought about this, I could see my own real-life example. As an undergraduate, I didn't have much time for my personal writing. Classes, work, and my social life as a late teen/young twenty-something kept me busy. As much as I had stories running through my mind, I rarely made time to actually write them down.

But I ended up finishing my degree a semester early and had eight full months off before starting graduate school. I was only working part-time in the evenings and my then-boyfriend worked full-time during the days, and as a result, I had a lot of free time I could have used for writing. I even had big ideas at the start of those eight months for how much progress I would make. Yet, when August rolled around and it was time to begin grad school, I hadn't done much writing at all.

Looking back now, I wonder what I actually did with all that free time. As much as I'd told myself I was going to "be productive," I didn't achieve much of what I'd hoped to. And I know now that's because I wasn't actively planning and scheduling time for writing. I woke up each morning hoping for the best, but before I knew it, the day had slipped away, and it was time to head to work.

I often joke that I get more done during periods where I'm objectively busier than when I have more free time. It seems counterintuitive, but the reality is that when I'm busier, I *have* to plan and prioritize to fit everything in. When I have more free time, I don't plan as carefully, and the result is often that I wake up without a plan and accomplish far less.

While there will always be seasons when we can't get as much writing done as we wish, the truth is that if you don't prioritize your writing when you're busy—if you don't fight to carve out even a little bit of time for it—you're unlikely to magically make time when life gets easier.

You Can Do Anything...But You Can't Do Everything

I heard this phrase several years ago now, and it was a huge mindset shift for me. Instead of feeling like a failure for not doing everything I wanted, I realized it's not that I *can't* do those things. It's simply that I can't do everything at once. Prioritizing is incredibly important.

If you're anything like me, you have more things you need and want to do each week than time to reasonably do them. For the longest time, I just threw everything on the list and hoped for the best. But week after week, I'd sit down with my planner on Sundays and berate myself for how little I'd accomplished. Then I'd roll everything, plus new tasks, into the next week and naively believe I'd somehow finish it all this time.

But finally, I got tired of letting myself down. One Sunday night, I sat down, took a hard look at my available time, and assigned each "must do" task an estimated time. When I added it all up, I was far in the red. No matter how much I *wanted* to get it all done, it simply wasn't possible. If I wanted to keep my sanity, I needed to prioritize.

Ultimately, no matter how much we wish we could do more, there's a limit to how much time we have each day. We may not like it, but we *need* to prioritize to be successful. That isn't to say you can't shift your priorities from week to week—for example, one week you might prioritize writing more than another—but you do need to be intentional about what you add to your to-do list and realistic about how much you expect of yourself.

Writing a novel is challenging, and it certainly requires a good amount of time and energy. If we don't make it a priority and intentionally set aside time for it, it's all too easy to let it slip to the bottom of the list. Sometimes, that means choosing writing over something else. Other times, it means accepting that writing will take a backseat to other life demands.

Reminding yourself that you can do anything but not everything is a powerful way to extend yourself grace. Even if you're not writing as much as you wish you could right now, it doesn't mean you aren't a writer. It simply means other priorities are taking center stage for the moment, and that's okay.

The key is to keep writing a priority in your mind and continue looking for time you can devote to it. Some weeks, that will be more time than others, but don't allow that to discourage you.

Consistent isn't the same as constant. Consistently showing up for your writing doesn't have to look like the same amount of time every single day. It might look like an hour a day one week and only one or two writing sessions the next. You'll still make progress. You're still showing up. You're still a writer.

Suggestions for Finding Writing Time

Finding time to write is always a bit of trial and error, especially during busy seasons. You might think waking up early will work, but in practice, you're just too tired to get anything done. That's okay. Keep trying different times and spaces to fit in your writing.

Even if something that used to work no longer does, that's okay too. Brainstorm and experiment until you find a new rhythm. Remember, you don't necessarily need long, uninterrupted stretches to make progress. Even twenty-minute chunks can be beneficial if you focus your efforts.

Sit down and brainstorm when you might fit in some writing, then test those time slots and pay attention to which ones are most productive. To get you started, here's a list of possible times you might reserve for writing:

- Wake up early before the kids/work

- Spend a chunk of time at your writing desk after dinner
- Write for a chunk of time after the kids go to bed
- Use your lunch break to write
- Write during nap time or implement "quiet time" for older kiddos
- Reserve weekend mornings for writing
- Write while making dinner or dictate while doing dishes
- Dictate in the car during commutes
- Write on public transportation
- Go to a coffee shop for a few hours on the weekends
- Write while the kids play in the bath or at the park
- Write during soccer practice, piano lessons, etc.

This isn't an exhaustive list, but hopefully it sparks ideas. The truth is that what works for one writer may or may not work for you, and you may need to try different possibilities before finding a good rhythm.

Don't get discouraged if you try something and it doesn't work. Keep experimenting. You'll find your groove.

Give Yourself Grace

The biggest piece of advice I can give is to allow yourself so much grace.

Yes, writing is a priority in your life—but beating yourself up for not meeting a goal isn't helpful. Life happens. Things will come up that interfere with writing time, no matter how carefully you plan. The important thing is to get back up the next day and try again.

You may not make progress as quickly as you'd like, but you're still moving closer to your goals.

Set realistic goals for yourself that account for everything else you have going on and be ready to readjust as needed. Even if you think it's realistic to write 3,000 words in a week, emergencies happen. Kids get sick. You get sick. Life throws curveballs. When that happens, it's okay to re-evaluate or even drop a goal altogether.

Don't beat yourself up for "failing." Instead, acknowledge your effort and keep moving forward.

Being kind to yourself will help you keep showing up for your writing. And every day you try again, you're building the writing life you dream of—one step at a time.

10

YOU DESERVE TIME TO WRITE
(YES, YOU)

ONE OF THE BIGGEST STRUGGLES I HEAR FROM WRITERS IS
not only that they feel they don't have time to write, but that
they don't believe they *deserve* to take time away from their
other obligations to pursue their writing. Hearing a writer tell
me they don't believe they deserve the time to work on their
writing will always be one of the most heartbreaking obstacles to
writing I encounter (and, if I'm being honest, one I sometimes
struggle with myself). While this feeling can stem from a variety
of factors, at its root is the belief that you, as a person, are not
worthy of joy, that you're not important enough to invest the
time needed to work toward a lifelong dream.

This breaks my heart because we are all worthy of living
lives that feel meaningful and bring us happiness. No matter
what other roles and responsibilities we carry, we ultimately
owe it to ourselves to create a life we love. And if being a writer
and creating stories is something that fills your life with joy and
meaning, then you absolutely, 1,000%, deserve the time to work
toward that goal.

Of course, this is a lot easier said than done. On a cognitive
level, many of us would probably agree that we're worthy of this.

But putting it into practice is another story. Setting boundaries and saying no to other things to prioritize writing time is an ongoing battle, and those thoughts of "I should be doing this instead" can creep in and slowly whittle away at our writing hours.

So, let's look at some of the causes of this belief—and how we can combat it.

Juggling Multiple Roles

The truth is, almost no writer is *solely* a writer. Unless someone has the luxury of not needing to earn an income, writing fiction isn't going to pay the bills, at least, not at first. While there are authors who eventually make writing their full-time job, many writers continue to create alongside other paid work or family responsibilities.

It's never easy juggling multiple roles, but it's something we do regularly throughout our lives. We work jobs while attending college. We parent while working full-time. We maintain households while supporting aging parents and nurturing relationships with our partners. Having multiple roles is simply part of life. So why, when it comes to writing, do we feel like we're juggling too much?

I think a lot of this stems from society's view of fiction writing. We don't view writing a novel with the same reverence we might view earning a graduate degree, for example. When we see a woman working full-time and raising young kids, then staying up late to write papers for school, we applaud her dedication to building a better life for herself and her children. But if that same woman spends her evenings writing a novel? Society is quick to label her selfish or irresponsible. After all, how could she take that time away from her children? *Clearly, she's not a good mother.* [Insert eye roll here.]

Unfortunately, because this is how society often views writing, it's all too easy for writers to internalize that view. When the only time we have to write is on weekends or evenings, we guilt-trip ourselves for taking that time away from our other responsibilities to pursue something that brings us meaning and joy. We internalize the idea that writing is frivolous, and to avoid feeling selfish, we put everything else ahead of our dreams.

But the trouble with this is that setting aside our dream of writing a book takes a toll on us, even if it's not immediately obvious. While there may be periods of time when we can't focus on writing as much as we'd like, pushing it aside altogether often leaves us resentful of our other responsibilities. If being a writer is a piece of who we are, then cutting off that piece will only leave us feeling incomplete.

It can be tempting to give up writing when other responsibilities consume your days. Believe me, I get it. I've often thought, "Wouldn't my life be so much easier if I wasn't worried about writing a novel on top of everything else?" I've even had stretches when I didn't write at all. But those stretches didn't make life easier. They made it emptier. Without the joy and meaning that writing brings me, I only felt more resentful and more guilty—guilty for letting go of something so important to me.

Rather than viewing our writing time as something selfish, we need to reframe the way we think about it. Ask yourself: *Would I still consider this selfish if I knew it would lead to a better life for myself and my loved ones?*

While writing may not guarantee financial success, it *does* guarantee a richer, more meaningful life. Pursuing something that brings you joy will always qualify as a worthwhile endeavor to me. If that doesn't feel true for you, ask yourself why.

Chances are, some self-limiting beliefs are influencing your thought processes here.

Writing with a Full-Time Job

One of the most common challenges I hear from writers is trying to write alongside a full-time job—which makes sense because most adult writers are also working in other careers. We need to afford rent and groceries somehow, right?

Many of my coaching clients have shared a common story: while they always dreamed of writing a book, the need (or desire) for a stable career pushed that dream to the back burner. Yet, even as they pursued other paths, the calling to write still nagged at them.

This resonates with my own journey and is one of the major reasons I became a book coach: to help writers realize that having a career and writing a book do not need to be mutually exclusive.

When I first committed to taking my writing seriously, I woke up early to write before work. When I started using my morning time to go to the gym instead, I shifted to writing on my lunch breaks at my office job. I dragged my laptop to the office every day and devoted that hour to my novel. It wasn't easy. There were days I just wanted to zone out for an hour instead of wrestling with my manuscript, and some days I barely made any progress. But looking back, I'm grateful I stuck with it. Having that routine helped me finish my debut novel and gave me the confidence to fully identify as a writer.

Where a lot of writers get tripped up is the belief that a "real writer" would be writing full-time. They question if they can call themselves a writer while working another job. But again, *most* writers aren't writing full-time. Reminding ourselves of this can help normalize our own experiences and help us feel less alone.

Another challenge is simply the exhaustion of working a demanding full-time job. Working forty hours (or more) per week is draining, even when we love our jobs. It can feel impossible to imagine adding writing on top of everything else. But if writing a book is truly important to you, finding the time—even in small pockets—will feel infinitely more rewarding than convincing yourself you can't do it.

Again, this comes down to mindset. Telling ourselves "I don't have time" is often just another self-limiting belief. I encourage you to sit down with your schedule and see where you might carve out a few writing sessions. It doesn't have to be huge blocks of time—even twenty minutes can be useful—but being intentional with your schedule and physically blocking off writing time as you would for an appointment makes it far more likely you'll follow through.

Many newer writers think they'll just write when "inspiration strikes" and therefore find the idea of scheduling their writing time counterintuitive. But the truth is, inspiration follows discipline. Developing a routine signals to your brain that it's time to be creative. If you wake up early and sit at your desk each day, eventually, even on the groggy mornings, your mind will meet you there.

Writing with a day job has its challenges, and it will likely take longer to finish your book than if you had uninterrupted time. But it's absolutely possible. The key is believing that writing will *enrich* your life, not burden it. While I won't pretend it's easy, I truly believe it's worth the effort.

Confronting Mom Guilt

Since I work primarily with women writers, the other huge obstacle my clients grapple with is mom guilt—and boy, do I understand this one.

As much as I love my son and wouldn't trade being a mom for anything, motherhood changed my life in ways I couldn't even comprehend before. Suddenly, most of my time wasn't mine anymore. Simple things, like making dinner or running an errand, are now more complex. There's no such thing as making dinner in peace and quiet (never mind *eating* in peace and quiet) or running into a store "real quick." Everything I do now requires making accommodations for the little guy I have tagging along with me.

And my writing life has been no exception.

Before having a child, I could write whenever I had time and motivation. But after becoming a mom, writing required layers of coordination: having time, having childcare, having the mental energy to be creative—which, let's be honest, is often lacking by the time 8 p.m. rolls around.

Finding time to write now means taking something away from my kid—either by locking myself in my office while Daddy handles bedtime, by writing while he's at daycare rather than picking him up earlier, or by prioritizing my writing over cleaning the house or making a homemade meal.

And...cue the mom guilt.

Mom guilt is incredibly powerful because we've been conditioned to believe that being a good mother means sacrificing our own wants and needs for our children's. And as much as we might be able to *logically* see the fault in that belief, it's very difficult for us to *emotionally* detach ourselves from it. Add in constant societal messages reinforcing it, and it's no wonder moms feel guilty for daring to pursue personal passions.

The typical counterargument to mom guilt is that doing things for ourselves is good for our children because it makes us happier and, therefore, better mothers. We shouldn't feel guilty for practicing self-care because doing so ensures we don't burn out *for our children*. And while that's true, it still doesn't actually address the problem of mom guilt.

The issue with this approach is that we're still feeding into the mentality that being a good mother means sacrificing for your child's benefit. We're still prioritizing children over mothers. We're still telling mothers that their children's wellbeing is more important than their own: they can take time away from their children to do things that will fuel them and help them to avoid burnout—but only because it has a payoff for their children as well.

But here's the thing. Yes, your kids need to see you doing something important to you, and yes, having a mother who is less stressed and happier because she does those things is good for them. But you deserve that for *you*, regardless of the fact it's good for your kids.

If we keep justifying our writing time by saying it's good for our kids, we're never truly addressing the real issue—the belief that we aren't worthy on our own. We're still only giving ourselves permission to write because our kids benefit from it.

But *we* deserve the benefit too. We are *worthy* of the time it takes to work on our writing simply because it's something that matters to us.

And here's the harsh reality: our kids may only be little for so long, and, of course, we want to soak up as much of that time as we can. But at the end of the day, you deserve to have something for yourself, too. You deserve to look back at your life when your kids are grown and know that you chased your own dreams even while you were busy helping them chase theirs.

You deserve the time to write because it makes *you* a happier and better person. End of sentence.

I know why people default to the first approach I outlined to defeating mom guilt. It's much easier to convince a mom to do something for herself by telling her it's good for her kids. As moms, we love our children and are willing to do anything for them. If you tell us that working on our writing will be better for them long-term, then we'll do it for that reason alone.

But if we don't address the root cause of mom guilt, then we're going to keep bumping up against it until we finally cave and let it consume us.

If mom guilt is a major struggle for you, it might take some deep work to overcome. But you are worthy of the time and space to chase your dreams. Being a mom doesn't erase your humanity. And if writing brings you joy, then you deserve to pursue it—for you. No justification required.

I know that seeking outside help to overcome these deep-seated beliefs might feel overwhelming (and might itself trigger guilt). I could sit here and tell you that getting help will make you a better mom. That it will benefit your kids in the long run.

But instead, I'll simply tell you this:

You deserve to feel worthy of pursuing your own dreams and passions.

End of sentence.

I KNOW that finding time for writing can be challenging. Especially when we're juggling a lot, it can be too easy for it to quietly slip to the back burner. But just because you have other roles and responsibilities doesn't mean you can't also be a writer. You deserve the time to write if it brings meaning to your life.

And you don't need to earn that time or justify it in any way. You deserve it simply because writing is a part of who you are— and you deserve happiness.

11

DEALING WITH UNSUPPORTIVE FAMILY AND FRIENDS

ONE OF THE MOST FRUSTRATING OBSTACLES I HEAR writers struggling with is a lack of support from family or friends. This lack of support can vary from not respecting a writer's dedicated time to write, to making blatantly hurtful comments about their dream of writing a book.

I've seen many writers hide their writing from those closest to them or even feel too scared to start because they're not receiving the respect and encouragement they need, and that will forever break my heart. After all, if someone you love has a dream—whether that's publishing a book or something else—why wouldn't you want to support it?

While it might seem obvious that our loved ones should want to support our dream of writing a book, it's unfortunately not always so clear-cut. There are many reasons others may not immediately jump on board to support your dreams, but at the end of the day, none of those reasons are actually about you or your writing. They stem from something else going on within them.

Still, it can't be denied that when those closest to us don't support our writing, it creates disappointment and hurt feelings. It can also make it more challenging for us to meet our goals.

So, how do we deal with it?

It's Not You, It's Them

Many writers lament that as soon as they share they're a writer, they're bombarded with a million questions—questions they may not feel comfortable or prepared to answer. Many writers are introverts, and writing is deeply personal, so answering these questions can feel exhausting, uncomfortable, and frustrating.

But I try to view these questions differently. Rather than assuming they're intrusive or judgmental, I often see them as coming from genuine curiosity. Going back to that survey I mentioned earlier, 80% of people dream of writing a book, yet only 15% ever start and even fewer get published. Many dream about it but never sit down to try. They may have been held back by the same fears and limiting beliefs we've discussed, yet it remains something they wish they could do or a talent they admire.

So, when we say we're writers, it makes sense that people get curious. They also likely have an image of what a writer looks like or how a writer lives, and meeting someone who claims that title gives them the chance to test those assumptions. (Side note: they typically want those assumptions confirmed—so don't be surprised if you burst their bubble. Just saying.)

Then there are the people whose questions truly *do* sound judgmental or insensitive. These individuals are likely feeling envious—maybe because you've achieved something they wish they could, or because you're pursuing a dream they've never had the courage to face. Their comments might sound like personal attacks, but they're usually not. Much more likely, those comments reflect internal struggles they haven't addressed. It just *feels* like it's about you.

When it's a stranger or casual acquaintance makes a cutting remark, it can sting, but it's usually easier to let it go. When the negativity comes from someone close to us, it feels more personal and is harder to ignore.

Daring to write a book is a brave endeavor. Many want to do it, but few follow through. Not only is finishing a manuscript something to celebrate, but even sharing your dream with someone else is a courageous act of vulnerability that deserves acknowledgment.

But it's exactly that vulnerability that triggers others. Many people have dreams they aren't showing up for—whether it's writing a book or something else—and your courage to chase after yours can feel threatening. After all, if you're doing it, what does it say about them that they're *not*? Your bravery to show up might hit on insecurities they're not ready to face. And just like writers sometimes make excuses not to write, others might try to belittle us rather than confront their own self-limiting beliefs.

Understanding this doesn't excuse their behavior, but it can help remind you that their attitude is about *them*, not you.

Share Your Feelings

While there may be some people in your life whose lack of support you can brush off, there may be others with whom you need to have a deeper conversation.

For example, you might be able to let go of a rude comment from your great-aunt you only see once a year. But if your significant other doesn't support your writing, that's going to create serious tension. Not only will it interfere with your ability to write, but it also hurts when someone so central to your life doesn't support a dream that's important to you.

This is where open and honest communication is key. Writing a book is already a vulnerable and courageous act, so build on that momentum. Dare to be honest with those who aren't showing up the way you need them to. These kinds of conversations never feel comfortable but avoiding them rarely proves helpful.

Before approaching the conversation, try journaling or talking with a friend or therapist to gain clarity on how this person's words or actions are affecting you. Jumping to accuse someone of being a horrible person probably won't result in the change you're hoping for. Instead, share your feelings and needs openly without attacking the other person. Keep in mind that their behavior might stem from something they're struggling with, and it's possible they haven't realized how hurtful their words or actions have been.

An honest conversation might help them see your perspective and make some changes. But if not, consider what boundaries you need to protect your peace. Maybe you decide not to talk about your writing with your mom. Or you might agree to disagree with your sister about your writing career.

The biggest thing to remember is that not writing is not the answer. If writing a book is a lifelong dream of yours and part of who you are, giving it up to smooth over a relationship will only leave you feeling resentful and hurting. Those in your life who can't support you may not come around, but they at least need to respect that this is a dream you're going to keep pursuing.

Changing who you are and abandoning your dreams is never the solution.

Concerns About Your Financial Security

One reason parents, in particular, might be unsupportive of your writing dream is concern for your financial future.

As we've discussed, writing isn't the most stable or lucrative career. It's not like studying medicine where there's a clearly defined path to financial success. Even completing an MFA in creative writing doesn't guarantee a specific job or salary. While there are ways to make money from creative writing, they don't typically come with a traditional benefits package like many parents hope for their children.

Many of our parents are from a generation where going to college meant you were guaranteed a stable, lifelong career—the kind of careers with pensions and long-term security. While those kinds of careers are increasingly rare, the creative path of a writer can sound unpredictable and risky to parents who grew up in that climate.

So, when you tell them you want to write a book, they might instantly imagine you quitting your job and moving to a cabin in the woods in an attempt to pen the Great American Novel. And while that might sound like a romantic notion, they're worrying how you'll pay rent and buy groceries. And those fears are often expressed through criticism and a lack of support for your dream.

If you suspect this is the root of your parents' concern, a calm, honest conversation might help ease some of their worries. Let them know you're pursuing your writing dream alongside other responsibilities or that you have a plan to support yourself through freelancing, teaching, or other income streams. Reassure them that you're not going to abandon your other obligations—you're just making space for something that matters deeply to you. That reassurance might help them relax and even share in your excitement.

Find a Support System

If those around you can't be supportive of your writing, I promise there are others out there who will be. Writing can feel lonely if you don't know people who understand the writing life, but thanks to the internet and social media, it's easier than ever to connect with people who do.

We'll talk more about writing communities in the next chapter, but for now, just know that finding other writers to talk with, learn from, and lean on can be a game-changer. While it won't erase the hurt of not being supported by those closest to you, having a support system of fellow writers can help you stay grounded and focused on your dream.

You're not the only one out there dreaming of writing a book. You're not silly or foolish for thinking that you, too, can publish a book readers will love. Others are out there doing it— and if they can, you can too.

Seek Professional Help

Sometimes, the lack of support from a loved one runs deeper than writing and points to a bigger issue within the relationship.

If someone's lack of support for your dream of writing a book is part of a larger pattern, it may be time to seek help. A coach or counselor can help you explore what's happening in the relationship and offer strategies for processing your emotions and moving forward.

You don't have to face this alone. Some situations are too big to navigate on our own, and getting outside help can make all the difference.

Keep Writing Anyway

My last bit of advice on this: *keep writing anyway*.

Again, not writing won't fix anything. Allowing someone else's disrespect to scare you away from your dream doesn't solve anything—it will only lead to resentment and loss.

Whatever's going on with the other people in your life, those are their issues to confront and work through. Your responsibility is to be honest about how you feel—and then keep writing.

Because truly: it's not you. It's them.

12

FINDING A WRITING COMMUNITY

WHEN I FIRST STARTED WRITING AS A KID, I DID SO IN complete isolation. I carried notebooks with me at school and would sneak in writing time whenever I could. This worked well for me then as I didn't need or want much input from others. I just wanted to create stories.

But as I grew older and began taking my writing more seriously, turning my focus toward completing a novel and eventually publication, writing in isolation wasn't as useful. Without other writers to critique my work or guide me on next steps, it was hard to know how to become a better writer.

I tried some online writing communities, but none felt quite right. I didn't find many writers who wrote stories similar to mine, or I found the members unwelcoming or a bit uppity. It wasn't until I discovered the Women's Fiction Writers Association (WFWA) that I found a community I clicked with—writers who understood the kinds of stories I was telling and could help me level up my craft.

Once I joined WFWA, I took advantage of every opportunity I could—attending workshops, seeking feedback, and soaking up all the knowledge available. I lurked the Facebook group to see what resources other writers were using, what questions they were asking, and what answers they were receiving.

The thing about writing is that as you improve and move into new phases of your journey, you encounter questions you never knew you had. Watching writers who were ahead of me on the path ask questions and get answers helped me absorb tons of valuable information, both for the present and for the road ahead.

For example, although I originally intended to pursue traditional publishing, I spent years absorbing knowledge about indie publishing through those communities. So, when I ultimately chose to go the indie route, I already had a foundation of information to draw from and didn't have to start from scratch.

Finding a community of supportive writers who understood my genre was the key to becoming a better writer and, eventually, to publishing my debut novel. I truly couldn't have done it without WFWA and the other communities I've joined over the years. That's why the first thing I tell anyone who wants to write a book is to find a writing community you connect with.

Beyond the guidance and resources, other writers understand the writing life in ways non-writers often can't, even if they support our dream to write. They understand the ups and downs of drafting, revising, and polishing a manuscript. They understand genre conventions and expectations. They understand the pros and cons of traditional versus indie publishing. They understand that being a writer takes so many different forms—whether it's a stay-at-home parent writing after the kids go to bed, someone squeezing in writing alongside a full-time job, or someone freelance copywriting to support their fiction dreams.

Every writer's life is different, but we can all connect over the highs and lows of the writing process. Having a community that gets it can make all the difference on the hard days—those days when carrying on feels impossible. On those days, your community will be there to support and encourage you. And, as discussed in the previous chapter, this can be particularly essential for writers who don't have family or friends supporting their writing ambitions.

Where to Find a Writing Community

So, now that I've (hopefully) convinced you that you need a writing community—where do you find one?

Finding a community can feel overwhelming, especially if you don't already know any other writers. As I mentioned above, when I first started searching out writing communities, I felt defeated. The ones I stumbled upon didn't feel right for one reason or another. But then I found WFWA, and it instantly felt welcoming and like the right place for me to grow as a writer.

My biggest advice here is not to give up. If you join a group and it doesn't feel like the right fit, that's okay. Keep searching. Thanks to social media and online platforms, there are countless writing communities out there. Sometimes it's just like dating— you have to try a few options before you find the right one.

A good place to start is by searching for established groups that focus on your genre. For example, I write women's fiction, so WFWA was a natural fit. If you write romance, you might explore the Contemporary Romance Writers or one of the many romance writing groups on Facebook. Starting with your genre can help you find like-minded writers who you already have something in common with.

From there, you might branch out into wider communities. There are so many different groups for writers that it would be hard to not find one (or several) that you fit with. Again, each group tends to have its own energy and dynamics, so don't be afraid to try a few before settling in. If you're nervous about jumping into a new group, observe for a bit before interacting yourself. Watching the types of posts others make—and the reactions and feedback they receive—can help you gauge whether the group is a supportive space for you.

Remember that a group should feel encouraging and constructive, not like a place where writers are torn down. If something feels off, don't force it. It's okay to move on.

Other social media platforms, such as Instagram and TikTok, can also be great ways to connect with fellow writers. While these platforms may not offer the same structure as formal groups, there are extremely welcoming and supportive communities in these spaces as well. Being active there can help you both connect with other writers and build your presence as a writer, which will be helpful down the road for publishing and marketing goals. It also helps reinforce your identity as a writer.

Writing conferences are another amazing way to meet other writers. These can be more expensive than online groups, but they come with built-in educational and networking opportunities. There are also virtual options that may be more budget friendly, and many have networking options as well as workshops.

And don't overlook your local writing communities! The internet is a wonderful place for building community, but it's also worth checking out what's happening in your own area. Local writers' groups, library events, or book festivals might offer the chance to meet fellow writers face to face. Having someone local to meet up and talk writing over coffee with can be incredibly grounding.

FINDING your writing community might involve a little trial and error, but once you do find the right fit, the impact can be transformational. Having a group of fellow writers to learn from, lean on, and celebrate with will help you improve your craft and feel more connected to your identity as a writer.

So, keep looking. Keep trying. The right community is out there. And it just might be the support system that changes everything.

13

THERE'S NO WRONG WAY TO BE A WRITER

A LITTLE WHILE BACK, I WROTE A POST FOR JANE Friedman's blog about adding meaningful words to lean manuscripts. The advice I shared came from my own experience being a lean writer—meaning my initial drafts of a manuscript typically come in well under the target word count for my genre, and I then go back through subsequent drafts to layer in descriptions, deepen scenes, and build out the narrative, which increases my word count. Even so, I tend to write on the shorter side. My debut novel, *The Serendipity of Catastrophe*, came in at about 71,000 words, which is considered short for a women's fiction novel.

As you might know, there's far more advice out there about how to *cut* words from manuscripts than how to add them. And at one point in my writing journey, this made me feel like I was falling short in some way. After all, if I were a *real* writer, wouldn't I have too many words to share, not too few?

It wasn't until I started connecting with other writers and found some who also admitted they wrote short drafts that I realized my writing style wasn't wrong; it was just different. Still, there are days when I question if my process isn't that of a real writer, and I have to admit I've even wondered if the shorter final word count of *The Serendipity of Catastrophe* might have deterred some of the agents I'd originally queried before deciding to indie publish.

For the most part, when those doubts creep in, I remind myself that I'm not alone and move on. But when I shared my blog post on lean manuscripts, several writers shared that they also wrote lean and worried they'd been doing something wrong. And that brought me back to those early days when I was so unsure, vulnerable, and deeply afraid I was getting it all wrong. It would have been easy for me to give up, convinced I wasn't doing this whole writing thing right, and never finish my novel. And it worries me that there may be young writers out there who give up too soon simply because their process doesn't look like someone else's.

Stop Comparing Yourself to Other Writers

It's easy to get caught up in comparing ourselves to our writing peers, especially early on. After all, we're looking for guidance, and it seems logical to emulate what other successful writers are doing.

But everyone's process looks a little different. As much as I love reading articles about my favorite authors and learning about their routines, as a young writer, it was easy to wonder if I was doing something wrong. I didn't wake up at 5 a.m., light a specific candle, sip my coffee from a particular mug, and crank out 3,000 words in one sitting, and those kinds of routines often left me feeling discouraged rather than inspired.

While it's interesting to get a behind-the-scenes look at how our favorite books were written, comparing ourselves to other writers—whether bestselling authors or fellow beginners—risks doing more harm than good. Just because one approach works for them doesn't mean it's the best one for us. Some writers thrive by waking up before dawn. Others do their best work at 10 p.m. If you write best late at night, that's your ideal time to write—even if no one else seems to say the same.

Another common trap is comparing where we are in our writing journey to where others are. Some writers work faster than others, some started earlier in their lives than others, and some might have a better knack for marketing their work. Just because someone else seems further along doesn't mean you're falling behind or doing it wrong. Everyone's life circumstances differ, and we rarely see the full picture when we're only looking at someone's highlight reel.

Looking to other writers for advice can absolutely be useful. Observing what works for others might help you brainstorm new strategies or approaches. But be mindful not to let comparison turn into discouragement. If something works for you, there's no need to change it. And if something doesn't resonate, don't force it. Pay attention to what others are doing but stay rooted in what works for *you*.

It's Never Too Late to Start Writing

One of the things I truly love about writing is it's never too late to start. Truly. I know writers who have been crafting stories their entire lives and others who didn't start writing until retirement.

But I also hear people say they'd love to write a novel, yet they wonder if it's too late. They worry they're too old to break into a new industry, that agents might overlook them because of their age, or that they don't have anything worth saying.

But these worries are nothing more than self-limiting beliefs. Writing isn't like taking up a sport where age becomes a barrier. In fact, the more you've lived, the more life experience you bring to your writing. With age often comes a deeper under-standing of relationships, emotions, and the world around us. I'd argue that you likely have *more* to say than someone just starting out in adulthood.

As for starting a publishing career later in life—I truly don't believe there's an expiration date. Again, writing isn't the kind of career where your skills diminish with age. Sure, there might be a learning curve in some areas, but if you can craft an engaging story readers resonate with, that's what matters. Any other challenges can be overcome by asking for help when needed.

At the end of the day, readers need your story—and *you're* the only one who can tell it. Don't let the fear of being "too old" discourage you. If writing and publishing a novel is a dream you've been holding onto, it's never too late to begin.

ULTIMATELY, if you write, you're a writer.

Whether your manuscripts are short and need building up or long and need trimming, you're a writer. Whether you write in long stretches or quick sprints, you're a writer. Whether you publish at 25 or 75, traditionally or independently, you're a writer.

The best way to be a writer is the way that works for *you*.

14

HOW BOOK COACHING CAN HELP

It's kind of funny considering that I *am* a book coach, but when I first started taking my writing seriously, I didn't even know what a book coach was. Maybe they didn't exist yet, or maybe I just didn't hadn't heard of them, but it wasn't something on my radar—and certainly not a career I ever envisioned for myself.

Part of this was because I, too, had been trapped by the belief that I needed a "real" job to be a responsible adult and support myself and my future family. I loved writing, but I knew it was a long shot to expect fiction to be a lucrative career, and I didn't see myself pursuing journalism or teaching English. Besides, I wanted to ensure my love for writing wasn't tainted by placing demands on it—as Elizabeth Gilbert puts it in *Big Magic*, "To yell at our creativity, saying, 'You must earn money for me!' is sort of like yelling at a cat; it has no idea what you're talking about, and all you're doing is scaring it away."[i]

So, instead, I pursued a career in mental health counseling, which eventually led me to life coaching. Still, I struggled to find work that truly fulfilled me. Then, when I was six months pregnant in the middle of the COVID-19 lockdown, I had what I can only describe as an "aha" moment. Sitting at my desk, I thought: *what I really want to do is help other writers write their stories.*

And then came a second, even more obvious thought that somehow hadn't occurred to me before: *Then why don't I just do that?*

Still, my immediate reaction was to let imposter syndrome creep in: after all, who was *I* to be a book coach? But then I walked myself through it. I had years of experience studying, practicing, and absorbing writing craft, and I had training in both counseling and coaching. All I needed to do was combine the two.

And then I cried tears of joy—because I had finally found a way to merge my love of writing with my career in a way that felt genuine and true to who I am. Helping others bring their stories to life and pursue their writing dreams truly brings me joy.

Do I believe writers *need* a book coach to write a novel? Of course not. I completed my debut novel without one, and many other writers do the same. But there are real benefits to working with a book coach, especially if writing a book has been on your bucket list for a while and you keep putting it off until next week, next month, or next year.

So, if you're wondering what book coaching could do for you, here are a few reasons you might consider it.

Accountability

Writing a book takes an incredible amount of dedication and effort, and it's up to *you* to hold yourself accountable. No one else is going to stand over your shoulder to make sure you're writing regularly. And this can be challenging for writers, new and experienced alike, especially when they hit a difficult part of the process.

One of the biggest benefits of working with a book coach is having someone to hold you accountable for reaching your goals. A book coach will help you set long-term goals (like finishing your manuscript) but will also help you break them into smaller, more manageable steps that feel realistic rather than overwhelming. They might help you set a weekly word count or time-based goal—and then check in to see how it's going. Knowing someone is checking in can help keep you motivated, and if you fall short, a coach can help you figure out why. Was the goal unrealistic? Did life get in the way? Either way, they'll help you troubleshoot and adjust moving forward.

But beyond tracking word counts, a book coach also holds you accountable for *not giving up on your dream*. Writing a book can feel daunting. And if no one else knows about your dream, it's easy to give up without feeling like much is lost. But when you work with a coach, you have someone in your corner —someone who will remind you why this goal matters, even when you forget.

Working with a book coach can help you finish what you started and finally write "The End" on your story.

Shorten Your Learning Curve

There's an abundance of writing advice out there—blogs, podcasts, craft books, online communities—and you absolutely *can* learn to write a good book by utilizing all of this. That's how I did it. But...it took me eight years from starting my manuscript to finally publishing my novel, and that's not counting two earlier unpublished manuscripts and countless half-finished stories.

While I learned a lot in that time, it included a lot of false starts, dead ends, and revisions I ultimately reversed, often because I was relying on advice that wasn't specific to *my* story. If I'd had a book coach guiding me from the start, I have no doubt I would have finished my novel sooner.

A book coach can help you narrow your focus, prioritize what to work on, and figure out which advice actually applies to your book. Because writing is subjective, it's common to get conflicting feedback and feel confused about which direction to go. A book coach offers a single, cohesive perspective—grounded in craft knowledge and a deep understanding of your unique vision—so you can move forward with confidence instead of second-guessing every choice.

A coach isn't going to magically make you a better writer or hand you a secret formula you can't find elsewhere. But they *can* guide you based on your specific strengths and needs, helping you reach your goals faster.

I like to think of it like working with a personal trainer. Sure, you can find workouts online and go to the gym yourself. But sorting through all that information can be overwhelming, and you're on your own to figure out what works. A personal trainer tailors a plan for you, helps you adjust when something isn't working, and gets you results more efficiently.

A book coach does the same. You still have to write the words, but they'll help you find the most effective path—and pivot if needed.

Identify and Overcome Your Self-Limiting Beliefs

As you might have guessed from the topic of this book, this is my favorite reason to work with a book coach.

While you might *know* what you need to do to write a book, you might still struggle to sit down and do it. That's often because of self-limiting beliefs getting in your way. And no matter how talented a writer you are, if you can't show up and do the work, you won't finish your novel.

A book coach can help you identity these beliefs more easily by offering an objective, outside perspective. My own coaching philosophy is to *start* with the mindset work—because more often than not, that's what's holding a writer back. But these beliefs are hard to see clearly when you're in the middle of them. Once identified, though, they can be addressed and worked through—freeing you up to write with clarity and confidence.

AGAIN, working with a book coach isn't a requirement for writing a good book. Plenty of writers do it without a coach. But if you've been trying to do this on your own and keep hitting walls, it might be worth exploring. A good coach can help you get unstuck, stay motivated, and bring your vision to life.

After all, the world needs your story—and only you can write it.

15

THE WORLD NEEDS YOUR BOOK

IF YOU'RE LIKE ME, YOU'VE HAD A LOVE FOR BOOKS SINCE the moment you could hold one in your hands. Maybe you knew from a young age that you wanted to be an author one day, or maybe this is a more recent dream. Either way, that little girl who once held and savored stories now dreams of creating one of her own. And you owe it to her to put in the work and write that story. Make that younger version of yourself proud.

A lot of people dream of writing a book "someday," but *now just isn't the time*. Work is demanding. The kids are young. A parent needs care. A partner just had surgery. The list goes on and on...and on. And I get it. Some seasons of life are busier and more chaotic than others.

But the problem with waiting for the "right" time is that it likely won't ever feel exactly right. There will always be something competing for your time and attention. There will always be more to learn before you *feel* ready. Rarely—if ever—do the stars align and the muse simply shows up to escort you to your writing desk.

But here's the thing: time is going to pass whether you're writing or not. Yes, there will be times when writing feels easier or more accessible. But being in a phase of life where you can only make slow progress doesn't mean you shouldn't pursue your goal at all. Slow and steady progress is still progress. Even if a year from now you only have a quarter of a manuscript written—that's a quarter more than you have today.

So, if not now, then when?

I won't lie to you and tell you that writing a book is easy. It's absolutely not. There will be days when you'll want to give up altogether. But those are the moments that make the payoff so rewarding. Knowing all that you overcame along the way—all the hours of drafting and revising, every time you thought about your characters like they were real people, every mental battle you fought and won—makes holding that finished story in your hands incredibly beautiful.

As we've explored throughout this book, it's often our own self-limiting beliefs—not outside circumstances—that hold us back from writing. And while it's never easy to acknowledge when we're sabotaging ourselves or to put in the work to change those thought patterns, the good news is this: you are in control of your own writing journey. If you're willing to do the work, you *can* write a book.

The biggest obstacle in your path is you.

You may wonder if you should put in that effort. And at the end of the day, only you can answer that for yourself. Only you know what this dream means to you and why you've held onto it. But I can tell you this: no matter how many books are already out in the world, none is *your* book. No one can tell the story that's on your heart in the way that you can. The world needs your story. And only you can write it.

Now that you have a better understanding of what might be holding you back, I challenge you to show up, do the work, shatter those self-limiting beliefs—and go write the book.

I'm cheering you on every step of the way.

WANT TO GO EVEN DEEPER?

If this book resonated with you and you're craving more support on your writing journey, I've created something extra just for you.

When you join my email list, you'll get exclusive access to private podcast episodes where I dive even deeper into the mindset challenges that keep writers stuck. These episodes are designed to help you build confidence, stay motivated, and finish your book.

Plus, you'll be the first to know about new blog posts, writing resources, and opportunities to work with me.

Sign up now and start rewiring your writing mindset—one episode at a time:

www.lisafellinger.com/writing-mindset-podcast

You don't have to face the mental roadblocks alone. Let's keep going, together.

ACKNOWLEDGMENTS

I never imagined myself writing nonfiction, let alone a book about writing mindset. But the more I worked with writers, the more I saw how often mindset, not skill or talent, was the true barrier to finishing a book. Writing this felt less like a choice and more like something I was meant to do—a way to offer encouragement, insight, and guidance to those who need it most.

This book wouldn't exist without the unwavering support of my family and friends, who believed in me long before I fully believed in myself. Thank you for supporting my dream of becoming a novelist and encouraging me on this journey as a book coach and editor. Your faith has given me the courage to continually shoot for the moon.

To my son: thank you for the gift of being your mom. While motherhood has changed my life in more ways than I ever could have imagined, it's also reminded me to never forget the joy, curiosity, and determination we all have as little kids. You've taught me that the hardest things are often the most meaningful, and just because something is challenging doesn't mean it's not worth pursuing.

And to my clients: thank you all for trusting me with your stories. It's been an absolute honor to walk alongside you on your writing journeys. You've inspired this book—and me—more than you know.

NOTES

Introduction

i. Quindlen, A. (2002, September 28). *Think you have a book in you? Think again.* The New York Times. https://www.nytimes.com/2002/09/28/opin ion/think-you-have-a-book-in-you-think-again.html

4. Does Writing Have to be Useful to be Worthwhile?

i. Merriam-Webster. (n.d.). *Useful.* In *Merriam-Webster.com dictionary.* Retrieved April 15, 2025, from https://www.merriam-webster.com/dictio nary/useful

5. What are Self-Limiting Beliefs?

i. Mother Jones. (2005, January). *Root causes: An interview with Wangari Maathai.* Mother Jones. https://www.motherjones.com/politics/2005/01/ root-causes-interview-wangari-maathai/

ii. Sangerma, E. (2021, October 26). *5 must-read Maya Angelou quotes to help you beat impostor syndrome.* Mind Cafe. https://medium.com/mind-cafe/5-must-read-maya-angelou-quotes-to-help-you-beat-impostor-syndrome-b197d1474b85

6. Overcoming Self-Limiting Beliefs

i. Hollis, R. (2022). *Girl, stop apologizing: A shame-free plan for embracing and achieving your goals* (Unabridged ed.) [Audiobook]. HarperAudio.

7. Why Do We Procrastinate?

i. Kramer, M. J., & Silver, M. (2006, November 22). *Jodi Picoult: You can't edit a blank page.* NPR. https://www.npr.org/2006/11/22/6524058/jodi-picoult-you-cant-edit-a-blank-page

14. How Book Coaching Can Help

i. Elizabeth Gilbert, *Big Magic: Creative Living Beyond Fear* (New York: Riverhead Books, 2016), 154.

ABOUT THE AUTHOR

Lisa is a professionally trained developmental editor, book coach, and published author. Her debut novel, *The Serendipity of Catastrophe*, was released in March 2024. With a background in mental health counseling and coaching, she brings a unique approach to supporting writers—blending craft experience with deep insight into the mindset challenges that can block creativity and progress.

As a book coach, Lisa helps writers overcome self-doubt, perfectionism, and other self-limiting beliefs that get in the way of finishing a novel. Her coaching supports the whole writer, addressing both the technical side of storytelling and the emotional work of claiming a writing identity, building confidence, and staying committed to the creative process. She's your writing cheerleader and trusted guide—always in your corner, encouraging you from start to finish.

As an editor, Lisa aims not only to strengthen your current manuscript but to equip you with lasting tools and insights to grow as a writer. Her counseling experience gives her a sharp understanding of character psychology and interpersonal dynamics, helping her clients craft stories that are layered, authentic, and emotionally resonant.

Lisa lives in Buffalo, New York, where she juggles motherhood, her own writing, and running a creative business with the help of a well-stocked coffee supply. When she's not cheering on her clients or revising her next novel, she's likely chasing after her son until bedtime. Evenings are for winding down with a good book, a sleepy cat, and just enough energy to make it through a chapter or two.

facebook.com/lisafellingereditor

instagram.com/lisafellingerwrites

pinterest.com/lisafellingereditor

linkedin.com/in/lisafellinger